# ABSOLUTE BEGINNER'S GUIDE TO PYTHON PROGRAMMING

### MASTER CODING QUICKLY WITH HANDS-ON, REAL-WORLD PROJECTS, STEP-BY-STEP GUIDANCE, AND COMPREHENSIVE LEARNING FOR ALL AGES

Stirling Hale

All rights reserved. No part of this publication may be reproduced, stored, or transmitted in any form or by any means, electronic, mechanical, photocopying, recording, scanning, or otherwise, without written permission from the publisher. It is illegal to copy this book, post it to a website, or distribute it by any other means without permission.

Copyright © 2024-2025 Wizardry Press, LLC
All rights reserved.

ISBN: 978-1-964520-00-1
(Paperback)

Python and the Python logos are trademarks or registered trademarks of the Python Software Foundation, used by Wizardry Press, LLC, with permission from the Foundation.

# WHAT THE MEDIA AND READERS ARE SAYING

 **digitaltrends** **A Gateway To The World of Coding**

*"Absolute Beginner's Guide to Python Programming* makes learning even more fun. It offers an immersive, hands-on experience through real-world projects, encouraging learners to code from day one rather than just absorb theory—it's truly an invitation into the world of coding."

https://www.digitaltrends.com/contributor-content/absolute-beginners-guide-to-python-programming-a-gateway-to-the-world-of-coding

 ★★★★★ **Perfect for Beginners—Helped Me Think Like an Engineer**
Verified Purchase

"This wasn't just a coding tutorial—it taught me how to think like an engineer."
— **Ian Seekell**, *Product Manager*

https://www.amazon.com/gp/customer-reviews/R330FM4AXP5TBL

 ★★★★★ **Start Sinking or Start Swimming**
Verified Purchase

"I once thought Python was overwhelming—this book changed that. I now see endless possibilities." — **Garrett Shearman**, *Content Creator*

https://www.amazon.com/gp/customer-reviews/R1CP1RA0IMM6N1

 ★★★★★ **Python Programming Just Got Accessible—Grandson Approved!**
Verified Purchase

"My grandson told me it's easy to follow and doesn't drown you in jargon. He even showed me his projects!" — **ShariC**, *Proud Grandparent*

https://www.amazon.com/gp/customer-reviews/R160S967UGOKDO

# What the Media and Readers Are Saying

### ★★★★★ From Clueless to Confident
Verified Purchase

"This book is like having a patient mentor. The real-world projects made coding enjoyable and confidence-boosting."  — ***Thomas Caine***, *First-Time Coder*

https://www.amazon.com/gp/customer-reviews/R3K0OF08F6MNXJ

### ★★★★★ Best Book for Beginners
Verified Purchase

"Better than any *For Dummies* book I've read. Even my teenage son followed along—and he loved it!"  — ***Lindsay***, *Tech-Savvy Parent*

https://www.amazon.com/gp/customer-reviews/R2VIHJS23X04Z9

### ★★★★★ Python for the Aspiring Nerds
Verified Purchase

"Whimsical, unintentionally hilarious, and inspiring... a delightful puzzle fit for the rest of us mere mortals."  — ***Captainron042***, *Verified Reviewer*

https://www.amazon.com/gp/customer-reviews/R81J2XGLP5X15

# ACKNOWLEDGMENTS

I want to express my deepest gratitude to the talented translators who helped make this book accessible to a broader audience.

To **Shreya Thapliyal**, thank you for your thoughtful and nuanced Hindi translation. Your dedication and attention to detail have made it possible for Hindi-speaking readers to enjoy and learn from this book. Your work didn't just translate the words—it captured the heart and spirit of the content, making it accessible to many more future programmers.

To **Eduardo Sánchez Castillo**, thank you for the outstanding Spanish translation of this book. Your skill and commitment ensured that Spanish-speaking readers can learn Python with ease and clarity. Your translation preserved both the educational intent and the enthusiasm of the original text, creating a smooth and inspiring learning experience.

Beyond the translation itself, your support and friendship at the beginning of this project made an invaluable contribution. Your involvement greatly enriched the development and global reach of this book.

Thank you both for your hard work and dedication to this project. Your efforts have not only expanded the reach of *Absolute Beginner's Guide to Python Programming*—you've helped open the door to this incredible technology and the world of Python for learners around the globe. Because of you, more people now have the chance to explore, create, grow, and better their lives—and the lives of those around them—through code.

If you're looking for one of the translated editions, you can find them here:

**Absolute Beginner's Guide to Python Programming**
https://www.amazon.com/dp/1964520002

**GUÍA absoluta para principiantes: Programación en Python**
*Coming Soon!*

**बिल्कुल Beginners के लिए Python Programming Guide**
https://www.amazon.com/dp/B0D9XRBM1C

# TABLE OF CONTENTS

**WHAT THE MEDIA AND READERS ARE SAYING** ..................................................... III
**ACKNOWLEDGMENTS** ............................................................................................... V
**TABLE OF CONTENTS** ............................................................................................. VII
**PREFACE – WHY YOU WANT TO READ THIS BOOK** ............................................ XV
**WORDS OF WISDOM** ............................................................................................. XVII
**THE ART OF FALLING: A PROGRAMMER'S JOURNEY TO MASTERY AND SUCCESS** ................................................................................................................... XIX
**INTRODUCTION** .......................................................................................................... 1
  WHY PYTHON? ............................................................................................................. 1
  WHAT MAKES PYTHON SPECIAL? ................................................................................. 1
  DISCOVERING PYTHON'S APPLICATIONS ...................................................................... 2
  GOALS OF THIS BOOK .................................................................................................. 2
  HOW TO USE THIS BOOK .............................................................................................. 2
  WHERE CAN I FIND THE SOURCE CODE FOR THIS BOOK? ............................................ 3
  FEEDBACK .................................................................................................................... 3
**CHAPTER 1: THE FIRST STEPS** ............................................................................... 5
  1.1 UNDERSTANDING THE PYTHON INTERPRETER ........................................................ 6
  1.2 CHOOSING AN IDE .................................................................................................. 6
  1.3 GETTING STARTED WITH VISUAL STUDIO CODE ..................................................... 8
  1.4 WINDOWS: INSTALLING PYTHON AND VS CODE .................................................... 8
  1.5 macOS: INSTALLING PYTHON AND VS CODE .......................................................... 9
  1.6 LINUX: INSTALLING PYTHON AND VS CODE .......................................................... 11
  1.7 CONFIGURING VISUAL STUDIO CODE FOR PYTHON DEVELOPMENT ..................... 11
  1.8 THE CLASSIC "HELLO, WORLD!" ........................................................................... 13
  1.9 EXECUTING A SCRIPT ............................................................................................ 15
  1.10 TAKING USER INPUT ........................................................................................... 16
  1.11 DISPLAYING OUTPUT .......................................................................................... 16
  1.12 CHAPTER SUMMARY ........................................................................................... 16
**CHAPTER 2: THE FOUNDATIONS OF PYTHON** ..................................................... 19
  2.1 VARIABLES AND DATA TYPES: THE BUILDING BLOCKS ........................................ 19
  2.2 RULES FOR NAMING VARIABLES ........................................................................... 21
  2.3 STRING FORMATTING IN PYTHON: F-STRINGS AND FORMAT() METHOD ................ 24
  2.4 UNDERSTANDING IMMUTABILITY ........................................................................... 27

TABLE OF CONTENTS

    2.5 COMMENTS: YOUR CODE'S ANNOTATION ............................................................. 28
    2.6 CONTROL STRUCTURES: MAKING DECISIONS IN YOUR CODE ........................... 29
    2.7 UNDERSTANDING PYTHON SYNTAX: INDENTATION AND THE COLON ................ 30
    2.8 CONSTANTS ...................................................................................................... 32
    2.9 `IF`, `ELIF`, AND `ELSE` ......................................................................................... 33
    2.10 CALCULATIONS IN PYTHON ............................................................................. 33
    2.11 PYTHON OPERATORS ...................................................................................... 34
    2.12 TERNARY CONDITIONAL EXPRESSION ............................................................. 38
    2.13 CHAPTER SUMMARY ....................................................................................... 39
    2.14 SUGGESTED EXERCISES .................................................................................. 40
    2.15 PROJECT: LOAN PAYMENT CALCULATOR ........................................................ 42

**CHAPTER 3: EXPLORING PYTHON WITH LOOPS AND COLLECTIONS ............... 45**

    3.1 LISTS ................................................................................................................ 45
    3.2 UNDERSTANDING MULTI-DIMENSIONAL ARRAYS IN PYTHON ........................... 47
    3.3 INTRODUCTION TO TUPLES .............................................................................. 49
    3.4 DICTIONARIES: MAPPING KEYS TO VALUES ...................................................... 50
    3.5 COMPARING DICTIONARIES TO LISTS AND TUPLES .......................................... 52
    3.6 SETS: UNLEASHING THE POTENTIAL OF UNIQUE COLLECTIONS ...................... 53
    3.7 PERFORMANCE CONSIDERATIONS ................................................................... 55
    3.8 SUMMARIZING COLLECTIONS .......................................................................... 55
    3.9 LOOPS: THE POWER OF REPETITION ................................................................ 56
    3.10 WHILE LOOPS ................................................................................................ 58
    3.11 LOOP CONTROL STATEMENTS ....................................................................... 58
    3.12 NESTING LOOPS ............................................................................................. 59
    3.13 CHAPTER SUMMARY ...................................................................................... 59
    3.14 SUGGESTED EXERCISES .................................................................................. 60
    3.15 PROJECT: BUILD A PYTHON QUIZ GAME ........................................................ 61

**CHAPTER 4: THE POWER OF FUNCTIONS, MODULES, PACKAGES AND LAMBDAS ............................................................................................................. 67**

    4.1 FUNCTIONS ...................................................................................................... 67
    4.2 SCOPE AND LIFETIME OF VARIABLES ............................................................... 69
    4.3 GLOBAL VARIABLES ......................................................................................... 69
    4.4 MODULES ........................................................................................................ 72
    4.5 PACKAGES ....................................................................................................... 73
    4.6 LAMBDA FUNCTIONS ...................................................................................... 75
    4.7 ENHANCING LAMBDA FUNCTIONS WITH `FILTER`, `MAP`, AND `SORTED` ........ 76
    4.8 CHAPTER SUMMARY ....................................................................................... 77
    4.9 SUGGESTED EXERCISES ................................................................................... 78
    4.10 PROJECT: TIC-TAC-TOE GAME ....................................................................... 79
    4.11 GAME DESIGN AND FLOW ............................................................................. 80

4.12 Step-by-Step Guide to Building the Game ..................................................81
4.13 Introducing an AI Opponent ......................................................................83
4.14 Step-by-Step Guide to Building the AI ......................................................84
4.15 Explore Advanced AI Techniques .............................................................85

## CHAPTER 5: DATA STORAGE: TEXT & JSON FILES ...............................89

5.1 Basic File Operations ..................................................................................89
5.2 File Paths and Directories ...........................................................................91
5.3 Using Paths Across Different Operating Systems .......................................91
5.4 Handling Errors with `try`/`except`/`finally` ...............................................92
5.6 Working with Text Files ..............................................................................93
5.7 Working with JSON Files ............................................................................95
5.8 Other Types of Structured Files ..................................................................98
5.9 Chapter Summary ......................................................................................101
5.10 Chapter Exercises ....................................................................................102
5.11 Chapter Project: Personal Expense Tracker ............................................104

## CHAPTER 6: NAVIGATING OBJECT-ORIENTED PROGRAMMING .........107

6.1 What are Classes and Objects? ..................................................................108
6.2 Define a Class ............................................................................................109
6.3 Creating and Using Objects .......................................................................110
6.4 Understanding Composition: Classes Within Classes ...............................110
6.5 Wrapping Up Encapsulation ......................................................................112
6.6 Embracing Inheritance ...............................................................................113
6.7 Wrapping up Inheritance ...........................................................................115
6.8 Exploring Polymorphism ...........................................................................115
6.9 Wrapping up Polymorphism ......................................................................116
6.10 Mastering Abstraction .............................................................................117
6.11 Abstract Classes vs Interfaces .................................................................118
6.12 Wrapping up Abstraction ........................................................................119
6.13 The Bigger Picture: What OOP Really Unlocks .....................................119
6.14 Chapter Summary ....................................................................................120
6.15 Chapter Exercises ....................................................................................120
6.15 Chapter Project: Enhanced Expense Tracker with OOP .........................122
6.17 Step-by-Step Guide: ................................................................................122

## CHAPTER 7: GRAPHICAL USER INTERFACES WITH TKINTER ............125

7.1 Verifying Tkinter's Availability .................................................................126
7.2 Troubleshooting Common Issues ..............................................................126
7.3 Your First Tkinter Application ..................................................................127

- 7.4 Layout Management .................................................................................. 129
- 7.5 Choosing the Right Layout Manager ....................................................... 133
- 7.6 Widgets: The Building Blocks of GUIs ..................................................... 133
- 7.7 Message Boxes ....................................................................................... 138
- 7.8 Event Handling in Tkinter ........................................................................ 141
- 7.9 Event Sequences and Modifiers .............................................................. 142
- 7.10 Advanced Widget Customization and Styles ........................................ 143
- 7.11 Using ttk (Themed Tk) for a Modern Look ............................................ 143
- 7.12 Dynamic Widget Updates ..................................................................... 144
- 7.13 Integrating External Data and Services in Tkinter Applications .......... 144
- 7.14 Deploying Tkinter Applications: Best Practices and Sharing with Users ......... 146
- 7.15 Chapter Summary ................................................................................. 148
- 7.16 Suggested Exercises ............................................................................. 148
- 7.17 Chapter Project – Convert Tic-Tac-Toe to Tkinter ................................ 150
- 7.18 Designing the Tic-Tac-Toe GUI ............................................................. 151
- 7.19 Review of Console Application ............................................................. 152
- 7.20 Updating the Main File - Initializing the Tkinter Loop .......................... 153
- 7.21 Step-by-Step Instructions ..................................................................... 154

## CHAPTER 8: EXPLORING THE FUTURE: WHERE TO GO FROM HERE ............... 157

- 8.1 Fields Where Python is Used .................................................................. 158
- 8.2 Web Development .................................................................................. 158
- 8.3 Data Science ........................................................................................... 158
- 8.4 Artificial Intelligence (AI) ........................................................................ 159
- 8.5 Scientific Computing .............................................................................. 160
- 8.6 Automation and Scripting ...................................................................... 160
- 8.7 Software Development ........................................................................... 161
- 8.8 Game Development ................................................................................ 161
- 8.9 Network Programming ........................................................................... 161
- 8.10 Finance .................................................................................................. 162
- 8.11 Chapter Summary ................................................................................. 162

## CONCLUSION .............................................................................................. 165

- Embrace the Endless Possibilities ................................................................ 165
- The Art of Falling .......................................................................................... 166
- Building a Strong Foundation ...................................................................... 166
- The Balance of Learning .............................................................................. 166
- Encouragement for the Future ..................................................................... 166
- Final Thoughts .............................................................................................. 166

## APPENDIX A: EXERCISE SOLUTIONS ......................................................... 167

- Chapter 2 Solutions ...................................................................................... 167

Chapter 3 Solutions ........................................................................................... 168
Chapter 4 Solutions ........................................................................................... 170
Chapter 5 Solutions ........................................................................................... 172
Chapter 6 Solutions ........................................................................................... 174
Chapter 7 Solutions ........................................................................................... 176

## APPENDIX B: GITHUB PRIMER FOR DOWNLOADING SOURCE CODE ............... 179

Accessing and Downloading Code from GitHub ........................................... 179
Tips for Using Downloaded Code ................................................................... 179
No GitHub Account Required ......................................................................... 180

## APPENDIX C: SELF-DOCUMENTING CODE: WRITING CODE THAT EXPLAINS ITSELF ................................................................................................................. 181

Key Characteristics of Self-Documenting Code ............................................ 181
Benefits of Self-Documenting Code ............................................................... 181

## APPENDIX D: CHOOSING THE RIGHT IDE ........................................................ 183

Visual Studio Code (VS Code) ....................................................................... 183
PyCharm ........................................................................................................... 183
Jupyter Notebook ............................................................................................. 184
Spyder ............................................................................................................... 184
Thonny .............................................................................................................. 184
IDLE (Python's Built-in IDE) ......................................................................... 185
PyDev (for Eclipse) ......................................................................................... 185
Anaconda Navigator ........................................................................................ 185

## GLOSSARY ............................................................................................................ 187

## MORE FROM WIZARDRY PRESS ........................................................................ 193

## INDEX .................................................................................................................. 195

# GET YOUR FREE EBOOK & AUDIOBOOK: UNLOCK YOUR PROGRAMMING CAREER POTENTIAL!

*Don't miss out—download your free guide now!*

Ready to take your programming career to the next level? As a thank-you for reading this Python guide, I'm excited to offer you my *Complete Career Guide for Entry-Level Software Engineers*.

This 170+ page guide is packed with actionable advice, real-world strategies, and insights to help you thrive in the programming industry, whether you're starting out, switching to a tech career, or looking to grow.

**Completely free in both *eBook and audiobook formats*!**

Scan the QR code or visit the link below to download your free copy:

https://levelup.wizardrypress.com/pbp

# Preface – Why You Want To Read This Book

Welcome to a journey that started back in 1976, in a middle school kid's reluctant tag-along to a university computer lab. My father, desperately trying yet again to connect with his difficult son, was taking a BASIC programming class at the university where he worked and insisted I come along.

To my father, it was a chance to share something new and hopefully connect with his son; to me, it seemed like a colossal waste of time. Yet, there it was. In Room 300 of the Clyde Engineering building stood a Digital PDP-8 mini-computer—a serious machine with eight terminals (all sharing 4k of RAM) that was not meant to be fun. But it was.

Against all odds, I discovered that learning could be exhilarating and far more engaging than anything else I had done. I hated school—I hated everything—but I loved this! A year later, the Radio Shack TRS-80 Model 1 came out, and I bought one with money earned delivering newspapers. That's how it started for me.

For many years, each technology book I read and every new tool I learned felt serious and somber, much like the stereotype of the typical programmer at the time—nerds who understood computers far better than they understood people. And I fit right in.

However, after decades in the field and many hard-earned lessons later, my perspective shifted. I began to understand and genuinely enjoy connecting with people. Now, the aspect of my job that I treasure the most is the people I meet and work with. This newfound appreciation for human connections has enriched my approach to technology, making me a better programmer, teacher, and collaborator.

This book is born from my enduring belief that technology can be fun because learning is inherently fun. Over my 40 years as a professional programmer, I've encountered numerous technologies, but Python stands out as one of the most enjoyable.

Writing this book has been one of my most challenging yet amusing projects. I've always enjoyed a good jest, and people are the best subjects for that. So, as you turn these pages and dive into learning Python, know that this book was written not just to educate but to have fun. I've embedded a bit of that mischievous spirit within these pages.

I hope you find as much joy in learning Python as I do in writing this book. My dream is that many of you will experience the same spark of excitement I felt in 1976.

# Preface – Why You Want To Read This Book

I began my career when the industry was still in diapers, and I've watched it grow into a rebellious (and immature) teenager. Just as I grew in my career, the technology industry evolved rapidly around me. With the advent of AI, I foresee growth in technology that will dwarf everything we've seen since the mid-'70s. What an exhilarating time to enter the field!

I hope that through these pages, you'll catch a glimpse of the immense possibilities that lie ahead. A career in technology is not just rewarding financially; it offers a quality of life and a level of satisfaction that are hard to match. You'll find yourself surrounded by innovative, passionate people who make ~~every~~ most days exciting and every challenge a puzzle to be solved.

So yes, I sincerely hope you get the spark! It's not just about learning a programming language—it's about embracing a vibrant future full of potential.

Python is very well positioned to take advantage of this future. And I hope you are part of it! Who knows where it might take you? I invite you to join this ever-evolving journey to learn, innovate, and maybe even disrupt as we venture into an exciting digital future.

As you embark on this journey into Python and technology, it's important to recognize that, like any career, it's not without its challenges. There are days filled with breakthroughs and triumphs, where everything clicks, and the code flows like poetry. But there are also days of frustration, where bugs seem untraceable and solutions elusive. It's a path of continuous learning and adaptation.

From my decades of experience, I can say that while the road has not always been smooth, it has been immensely rewarding. Comparing notes with friends and family in other fields, I realize I've had it quite good. The satisfaction of solving complex problems, the joy of building something out of nothing but lines of code, and the camaraderie found in teams of like-minded thinkers have all made this journey worthwhile. As a co-worker, Blake, pointed out to me the other day, "We really hit the jackpot with this career." And Blake wasn't referring to money.

So, yes, the field of technology has its ups and downs, but the highs are often high enough to make the lows more than manageable (think of it as a package deal). It's a career that continually challenges and rewards in equal measure, offering a dynamic and fulfilling path for those who choose to take it. Come join us, we could really use you!

-Stirling Hale, P$^4$
"Perpetually Perplexed Python Programmer"

# WORDS OF WISDOM

Often, the greatest barrier to acquiring knowledge is the belief that we already possess it, leading us to overlook the need for further learning.

---

Always stay humble and hungry for knowledge— or become irrelevant.

---

This I know: The more I know, the more I know that I don't know.

---

Don't confuse brilliance with wisdom. Wisdom comes from experience, not brilliance. Use your brilliance to get experience and become wise.

---

The definition of a programmer is a machine that converts pizza into code.

---

Life is like a game composed of doors of opportunity. Each action you take or refrain from taking will open or close doors. The trick is to make the right choices that open the doors you desire while closing the ones you'd rather avoid. Not making a choice is a choice in itself that closes doors.

---

There is a vast amount of knowledge out there for you to acquire. Be patient with yourself and others as you grow to acquire it. All knowledge, great or small, is achieved, line-upon-line, precept-upon-precept, concept-upon-concept. Here a little, there a little. You still haven't scratched the surface until you have acquired much of it. So, don't get a big head and get back to learning.

---

The decisions you make now will eventually come back to meet you. So, whether good or bad, you get to reap the rewards of the decisions you make. *–unknown author*

# THE ART OF FALLING:
## A PROGRAMMER'S JOURNEY TO MASTERY AND SUCCESS

Just as infants learn to walk, every programmer begins their journey amid uncertainty and frequent stumbles. Each fall and setback is not merely **part of the process**—it's essential to your growth. Imagine if an infant ceased trying after a few falls. They would never discover the confidence and freedom that comes with walking and eventually running.

Like these determined young learners, when you face challenges in programming—or any endeavor—remember that **falling is not failing**. It's a crucial pause, a lesson that is integral to the journey toward proficiency. Every programmer will face moments akin to being thrown off a horse. The key isn't just in mustering the courage to get back on, but to take a moment to reflect on why the fall happened and to recognize and even celebrate the growth you have already achieved, between falls.

Too often, beginners believe that mastery belongs only to those with natural talent. That's a dangerous myth. **Skill isn't inherited; it's built**—one mistake, one lesson, one small success at a time. Every great programmer you admire was once a beginner at some point. They stumbled through the basics and questioned their abilities like everyone else (it's just that some people are better at hiding it).

So, as you remount the horse, focus not on the sting of the fall but on the **invaluable lessons gained**. Recognizing and even celebrating your growth and lessons for each challenge is a stepping stone toward mastery. Indeed, becoming skilled isn't about avoiding falls but embracing them and learning to rise from them with renewed insight and determination.

# The Art of Falling:
## A Programmer's Journey to Mastery and Success

Beware of perfectionism. It's tempting to believe that if your work isn't flawless, it isn't good enough. But perfectionism can paralyze progress. **Growth demands action—and action is often imperfect**. If you can't look back at the code you wrote six months ago and say, "If I were writing that now, I could do it better," then maybe you're not growing.

Along this journey, remember that **no one walks alone**. The presence of mentors, friends, and a supportive community can illuminate paths that were once hidden and make the burden of setbacks lighter. These supporters are not just bystanders but active participants in your journey, offering guidance, encouragement, and sometimes the necessary push to help you move forward. They enrich your journey, ensuring that each step is informed by collective wisdom and shared experiences.

I dare you to name a single growth you've experienced that didn't come with a challenge. **Embrace these challenges, and cherish those who help you face them**, for they are the true catalysts of personal and professional development—hidden in plain sight, as essential as the very steps an infant takes towards their first run.

**The road ahead won't always be clear, and it won't always be easy. But it will be yours** — every fall, every rise, every triumph uniquely yours. And someday, you'll look back and realize that every stumble shaped you into someone stronger than you ever imagined, walking a path you could never have foreseen when you first began.

# Introduction

Welcome to the world of Python programming, where simplicity meets immense power. Celebrated for its straightforward syntax, Python is quickly grasped by newcomers yet robust enough for complex software development, making it a favorite among hobbyists and professional developers alike.

## Why Python?

Python consistently ranks as one of the most popular programming languages globally and is known for its versatility across various fields. Its clean and readable syntax not only makes programming more intuitive but also lowers the barrier to entry for newcomers. Whether you are eyeing a career in technology or seeking a rewarding hobby, Python provides a solid foundation that will serve you well into the future.

## What Makes Python Special?

- **Readability and Simplicity**: Python's code reads almost like English, focusing your attention on solving problems rather than navigating syntax nuances.
- **Versatile Application**: Python's powerful libraries and frameworks cater to a wide range of applications from web development with Django to machine learning with TensorFlow.
- **Immediate Execution**: As an interpreted language, Python allows for rapid testing and iteration, ideal for prototyping and experimental projects.

- **Strong Community Support**: The Python community offers beginners ample resources, guidance, and tools to enhance their programming journey.

## Discovering Python's Applications

Python's flexibility makes it invaluable in numerous domains:

- **Web Development**: Python simplifies web application creation using frameworks like Django, emphasizing security, scalability, and maintainability.
- **Data Science and AI**: Tools like Pandas and TensorFlow make Python a leader in turning complex datasets into actionable insights.
- **Automation**: Python streamlines business processes and network operations, reducing effort through automation.
- **Broad Impact**: Python excels in scientific computing, education, and finance, proving its utility in diverse challenges.

For a deeper exploration of Python's capabilities, please refer to the appendix, which provides an extended list of libraries and frameworks for each application area.

## Goals of This Book

This guide aims to transform you from a Python novice to a proficient programmer through practical projects that simulate real-world challenges:

- **Master Fundamental Concepts**: Gain a strong grasp of Python's basics, which is essential for any programming task.
- **Engage with Hands-on Projects**: Apply what you learn to cement your knowledge and skills.
- **Develop Problem-Solving Abilities**: Enhance your ability to tackle technical problems creatively and efficiently.
- **Learn Best Practices**: Adopt programming best practices for clean, efficient, and maintainable code.

## How to Use This Book

Maximize your learning by actively engaging with the content:

- **Practical Interaction**: Dive into each example and project for invaluable hands-on experience.
- **Nerd Notes**: Watch for "Nerd Notes" that delve into Python's nuances and programming tidbits for those eager to explore beyond the basics.

- **Accessing Source Code**: All project files and example codes are available on GitHub, allowing you to replicate and experiment with the codes firsthand.
- **Keep It Fun**: Embrace the challenges and creativity that programming with Python allows. Enjoy the process as you build and learn.

By the end of this journey, you'll not only understand Python but also appreciate how to apply it effectively in various contexts, setting the stage for further exploration and career development.

## Where Can I Find the Source Code for This Book?

The complete source code for this book is available on GitHub. This includes exercise files and full solutions for chapter projects, organized in a repository with separate folders for each chapter. You do not need a GitHub account to access these files.

GitHub
Wizardry Press – Beginners Guide to Python Repository
https://github.com/wizardrypress/Beginners_Guide_To_Python

The Appendix provides a primer on the basics of navigating the repository, downloading files, and utilizing the available resources for those unfamiliar with GitHub.

Use this repository as a companion to the book to practice and apply what you learn in each chapter.

## Feedback

I truly value your input as a reader, and your feedback helps me improve my work for future editions. If you have any thoughts, suggestions, or even constructive criticisms, I would love to hear from you. Please feel free to reach out to me at **feedback@wizardrypress.com**. Whether it's a question, a new idea, or just a note on what worked well or didn't, your voice matters and is greatly appreciated.

Thank you for taking the time to share your insights!

# Chapter 1: The First Steps

Welcome to your first steps into the world of Python programming! Whether you're looking to shift careers, enhance your skill set, or simply explore a new hobby, Python offers a world of possibilities that can transform your ideas into reality through coding. Imagine creating your own applications, automating mundane tasks, or even analyzing complex data sets—all of this starts with the fundamentals you'll learn right here.

Python is renowned for its simplicity and readability, making it an ideal starting point for those new to programming. Its versatility is celebrated worldwide, with professionals using it from web development to artificial intelligence, making it one of the most in-demand skills in today's tech job market. But beyond these practical reasons to learn Python, there's a deeper joy in programming. Like solving a complex puzzle, each line of code you write builds towards a solution crafted by your own logic and creativity.

In this chapter, we will guide you through setting up Python and an Integrated Development Environment (IDE) on your computer. We've got you covered whether you're using Windows, macOS, or Linux. We'll also dive into writing your very first Python program. By the end of this chapter, you will have the tools set up and understand the basics of Python's syntax and see your first code come to life!

Chapter 1: The First Steps

Let's embark on this coding adventure together, turning curiosity into knowledge and problems into solutions, one line of Python at a time. Embrace this journey with patience and persistence, and you'll discover the rewarding process of learning to program—gaining skills that will serve you for a lifetime.

## 1.1 Understanding the Python Interpreter

At its core, the Python interpreter is a program that reads and executes Python code directly. Think of it as a translator who reads your Python instructions (the code) and immediately carries out what you've told it to do step-by-step. This process happens every time you run a Python script, and it allows you to see the results of your code almost instantly.

### Interpreter vs. Compiler

To put this in perspective, let's compare it to another common way that programming languages run, which involves a compiler:

- **Interpreted Languages (like Python or JavaScript):** These languages use an interpreter that runs through your script, reading and executing one line at a time. This method is generally slower than compiled languages but offers more flexibility and easier debugging. You can make changes to your code and immediately see the effects the next time you run your script.

- **Compiled Languages (like C, C++, C#, or Java):** Compiled languages use a compiler, a tool that first takes your entire program and transforms it into machine code, which your computer's processor can execute directly. This process happens before you run the actual program. The advantage is that once your program is compiled, it can run very fast and efficiently. However, every time you make a change to your source code, you must recompile it before running the program again, which can slow down the development process.

Python simplifies the trial-and-error process by using an interpreter, making it an excellent choice for beginners and for situations where you want to write and test code quickly. This immediate feedback loop is invaluable for learning and experimenting with new programming concepts.

## 1.2 Choosing an IDE

In the world of Python programming, choosing the right Integrated Development Environment (IDE) can significantly impact your productivity and enjoyment. The ideal IDE becomes your digital workshop, providing the tools and environment to craft elegant code. To help you find the perfect fit, here's a quick comparison of popular options:

- **Visual Studio Code (VS Code):** Microsoft's VS Code has taken the programming world by storm. It is highly customizable and versatile and caters to a wide range of programming languages, including Python. Its lightweight nature makes it incredibly fast, ideal for those who prefer a minimalist approach. However, to unlock its full potential for Python development, you'll need to install extensions for features like linting, debugging, and code completion. Later in this chapter, we walk you through installing VS Code.

- **PyCharm:** Developed by JetBrains, PyCharm is often considered the gold standard for professional Python development. Its comprehensive suite of tools includes intelligent code completion, powerful refactoring capabilities, and integrated testing support. PyCharm's polished and user-friendly interface makes it easy to navigate, even for complex projects. However, its extensive features can make it resource-intensive on less powerful machines. This happens to be my personal preference. Mainly because I use other JetBrains IDEs for other languages.

- **Jupyter Notebooks:** Jupyter Notebooks offers a unique web-based environment that is perfectly suited for data science and analysis. Their interactive nature allows you to seamlessly blend code, visualizations, and explanatory text within a single document. This makes them ideal for experimentation, teaching, and sharing your findings. However, Jupyter Notebooks might not be the most efficient choice for large-scale software development projects.

- **PyDev (Eclipse Plugin):** PyDev brings Python power to the Eclipse ecosystem. It offers robust features, including code analysis, refactoring, debugging, and Django integration. Its high degree of customizability allows you to tailor your workflow to perfection. However, if you're not already familiar with Eclipse, the learning curve can be steep.

- **IDLE:** Included with Python itself, IDLE is the simplest IDE on this list. It's perfect for beginners and small scripts, providing a straightforward interface and basic features like syntax highlighting and debugging. While it lacks the advanced capabilities of other IDEs, its ease of use makes it a great starting point for those new to Python.

For a more in-depth comparison of these and other IDEs, including information on licensing, version control integration, debugging tools, community support, and documentation, refer to the Appendix. By carefully considering your specific needs and preferences, you can choose an IDE that empowers you to write better Python code more efficiently.

## Freedom to Choose

It is important to note that this book's examples, exercises, and projects do not depend on any specific IDE. Any IDEs listed here, in the Appendix, or even others not mentioned, will work equally well.

Chapter 1: The First Steps

## 1.3 Getting Started with Visual Studio Code

Since this is likely your first experience programming, we will guide you through installing and setting up Visual Studio Code to help you get started smoothly. We'll walk through the basics of using it, such as setting up your Python environment, understanding the interface, and running your first script. This step-by-step introduction will ensure you have the tools ready to dive into the exciting world of Python programming.

By focusing on Visual Studio Code, we aim to provide a stable and flexible foundation for your programming journey while ensuring you have the freedom to explore and switch to another IDE as you become more comfortable with Python and better understand your personal or project-specific needs.

## 1.4 Windows: Installing Python and VS Code

### Steps to Install Python

1. **Open your web browser** and go to the official Python website:

    Python.org
   https://www.python.org/downloads

2. **Download the latest Python installer for Windows** by finding the latest release (which is 3.12.3 at the time of writing this book)

   | Release version | Release date | | Click for more |
   | --- | --- | --- | --- |
   | Python 3.12.3 | April 9, 2024 | Download | Release Notes |
   | Python 3.11.9 | April 2, 2024 | Download | Release Notes |
   | Python 3.10.14 | March 19, 2024 | Download | Release Notes |
   | Python 3.9.19 | March 19, 2024 | Download | Release Notes |
   | Python 3.8.19 | March 19, 2024 | Download | Release Notes |

   - The next web page will display all kinds of information about the release you selected. Scroll down to the "**Files**" section.
   - Select either "**Windows Installer (64-bit)**" or "**Windows Installer (32-bit)**", whichever is appropriate for your computer. If you're unsure, start with "**Windows Installer (64-bit)**".

3. **Run the installer** once it's downloaded.

- Make sure to check the box that says "**Add python.exe to PATH**" during installation. This ensures that Python is added to your system's PATH environment variable, making it easier to run Python from the command prompt.
- But you will need to reboot your computer for changes to your system's PATH to take effect.

4. **Follow the installation wizard** instructions, and Python will be installed on your Windows machine.

## Steps to Install of VS Code

1. Open your web browser and navigate to the official VS Code website:

   Microsoft
   Visual Studio Code Download
   https://code.visualstudio.com/download

2. Download the latest Visual Studio Code installer for Windows by clicking on the "x64" or "Arm64" (depending on your computer) button. This will download the .exe installer suitable for Windows.

3. Run the installer once it's downloaded. Execute the downloaded .exe file. If prompted by Windows, confirm that you trust the source of the application to proceed with the installation.

4. Follow the installation wizard instructions. During installation, you can choose options such as adding a desktop icon, adding 'Open with Code' actions in the file context menu, and registering Visual Studio Code as the default editor for supported file types.

5. Complete the installation and launch Visual Studio Code. Once the installation is complete, you can launch Visual Studio Code directly from the installer's last screen or from the Start menu.

With Visual Studio Code installed on your Windows machine, you can begin configuring it by installing extensions such as the Python extension for Python development. This extension will enhance the coding experience by providing features like IntelliSense, linting, and debugging capabilities.

Next, jump to the section titled "Configuring Visual Studio Code for Python Development."

## 1.5 macOS: Installing Python and VS Code

### Steps to Install of Python

1. **Open your web browser** and go to the official Python website:

# Chapter 1: The First Steps

**Python.org Downloads**
https://www.python.org/downloads/mac-osx

2. **Download the latest Python installer for macOS** by clicking on the "Download macOS X.XX installer" link.

   - **Once it's downloaded, run the installer**. The installer package will have a `.pkg` extension. Double-click it to start the installation.
   - **Follow the installation wizard** instructions, and Python will be installed on your macOS.

## Steps to Install of VS Code

1. Open Your Web Browser and go to the official Visual Studio Code website to access the latest version:

Microsoft
Visual Studio Code Download
https://code.visualstudio.com/download

2. Download Visual Studio Code for macOS. Click on the "Download for Mac" button. This will download a `.zip` file containing the Visual Studio Code installer.

3. Install Visual Studio Code:

   - Once the download is complete, open your 'Downloads' folder and locate the `.zip` file.
   - Double-click the `.zip` file to extract the application.
   - Drag the Visual Studio Code application to your 'Applications' folder to install it. This action copies Visual Studio Code into your Applications, making it available in the Launchpad.

4. Launch Visual Studio Code:

   - Open your 'Applications' folder and double-click on the Visual Studio Code icon to launch it.
   - You may see a warning the first time you run Visual Studio Code as it is downloaded from the Internet. Click "Open" to continue.

Next, jump to the section titled "Configuring Visual Studio Code for Python Development."

## 1.6 Linux: Installing Python and VS Code

### Steps to Install of Python

Most Linux distributions come with Python pre-installed. To check if Python is already installed on your Linux system, open a terminal and type:

```
python3 --version
```

If Python 3 is not installed, follow these steps to install it:

*Ubuntu/Debian (including Raspberry Pi):*

```
sudo apt update
sudo apt install python3
```

*Fedora:*

```
sudo dnf install python3
```

*CentOS/RHEL:*

```
sudo yum install python3
```

### Verifying Your Python Installation

To verify that Python is correctly installed on your system, open a terminal (or command prompt on Windows) and type:

```
python3 --version
```

You should see the Python version number displayed.

## 1.7 Configuring Visual Studio Code for Python Development

Visual Studio Code (VS Code) is a versatile and powerful IDE that supports multiple programming languages and development environments. This flexibility makes it an invaluable tool for developers who work across various technology stacks. However, optimizing VS Code for Python development requires a specific configuration to tailor its environment to Python's needs.

To begin programming with Python in VS Code, follow these steps to ensure the editor is properly configured:

1. **Install the Python Extension:**
    - Open VS Code and navigate to the Extensions view by clicking on the square icon in the sidebar or pressing `Ctrl+Shift+X` (Windows/Linux) or `Cmd+Shift+X` (macOS).
    - Search for the official Python extension published by Microsoft and click 'Install'. This extension adds rich support for the Python language, including features like IntelliSense, linting, debugging, code navigation, code formatting, refactoring, and more.

2. **Select the Python Interpreter:**
    - Once the Python extension is installed, you can select which Python interpreter to use. To do this, open the Command Palette by pressing `Ctrl+Shift+P` (Windows/Linux) or `Cmd+Shift+P` (macOS), type 'Python: Select Interpreter' and press Enter.
    - Choose the interpreter you wish to use from the list. If you have multiple Python versions installed or use a virtual environment, you can specify which VS Code should use for your project.

3. **Set Up the Integrated Terminal (Optional)**:
    - Visual Studio Code has an integrated terminal that can be used to run shell commands directly within the editor. Open it by selecting `View > Terminal` or using the shortcut `Ctrl+`` (backtick).
    - Configure the default shell by clicking on the dropdown menu in the terminal window and selecting "Select Default Shell."

4. **Configure Version Control Integration**:
    - All of the source code for this book is downloadable from GitHub, which integrates nicely with Visual Studio Code through Git.

    *GitHub*
    *Wizardry Press – Beginners Guide To Python Repository*
    https://github.com/wizardrypress/Beginners_Guide_To_Python

    - Visual Studio Code supports Git out of the box. Set up Git by navigating to the Source Control menu (the branch icon on the sidebar), where you can initialize repositories, commit changes, and push or pull from remote repositories.
    - Ensure Git is installed on your system and properly configured in the Visual Studio Code settings to link with your repositories.

5. **Customize Workspaces**:
    - Workspaces in Visual Studio Code allow you to organize and save your project settings and debugging configurations. To create a new workspace, select `File >`

`Save Workspace As…` and specify the folder and workspace settings according to your project needs.

6. **Learn Helpful Shortcuts:**
   - To increase productivity, familiarize yourself with Visual Studio Code's shortcuts. Access the shortcut list by selecting `Help > Keyboard Shortcut Reference` or searching for specific actions in the Command Palette (`Cmd+Shift+P` on macOS, `Ctrl+Shift+P` on Windows/Linux).

7. **Explore Additional Features:**
   - Take time to explore features such as debugging tools, live share capabilities for collaborative coding, and the ability to connect to remote development environments directly from Visual Studio Code.

By following these steps, you can optimize Visual Studio Code to suit your development style and project requirements. This setup ensures you have a powerful, customized tool ready to tackle any programming task efficiently.

## 1.8 The Classic "Hello, World!"

So, you've got your Python environment ready, and it's about time we put it to good use. Writing your first Python script is a rite of passage, akin to a musician penning their first song or a chef creating their first signature dish. It's your introduction to the world of programming—a world where you communicate with your computer, instructing it to perform tasks, big and small. Let's roll up our sleeves and get started.

### What is a Program or Script?

In the digital realm, a script acts as a set of instructions for your computer, much like a playbook in sports. It's a file filled with commands that tell your machine exactly what to do, from displaying text to conducting complex data operations. Think of a Python script as a recipe where each line of code adds a new flavor, making it not only palatable for the computer but also readable and simple for humans. This clarity is why Python is a prime choice for automation tasks such as sending emails, scraping websites, or managing files.

### First Steps with Visual Studio Code (VS Code)

VS Code is more than just a text editor; it's a robust environment equipped with debugging, task running, and version control capabilities, essential for both novices and experienced developers.

1. **Launching *Visual* Studio Code:**

Start VS Code from your desktop shortcut, Start menu, or Applications folder.

2. **Creating a New Python File:**

   Click the "New File" icon and save the file with a `.py` extension, like `hello.py`. This extension signals that the file is a Python script.

3. **Writing Your First Python Code:**

   In your new file, enter the following line of code:

   ```
   print("Hello, Python World!")
   ```

   This line tells Python to use the `print()` function to display the message "Hello, Python World!" in the console.

 **The Ancient Ritual of Hello World**

*The tradition of the "Hello World" program finds its roots in the book "The C Programming Language" by Brian Kernighan and Dennis Ritchie. Brian Kernighan had introduced a version of the program even before this, in his 1972 tutorial for the B programming language. The B language (like A before it), never left Bell Labs, but they were the foundation for C, which was the foundation for C++, Java, C# and just about every other modern language, including Python. And every one of those languages had their own version of "Hello World."*

*Every time you code 'Hello World,' you're donning your digital armor, paying homage to the ancient code warriors before you.*

*From the secretive halls of Bell Labs, where the B language whispered the first 'hello', to the mighty empire of C and beyond, these linguistic architects laid the groundwork for our modern coding conquests.*

*By continuing this tradition, you join the ranks of these illustrious forebears, a modern warrior in the age-old fellowship of programmers. So, as you type out these sacred words, remember—you're not just coding; you're keeping the flames of tradition alive, one 'Hello World' at a time!*

## Running Your Python Script

To execute your script in VS Code:

1. Open the integrated terminal by selecting `View > Terminal` from the top menu or pressing `Ctrl+`` (backtick).

2. Type `python hello.py` and hit Enter. You should see "Hello, Python World!" appear in the terminal, confirming your script works as expected.

## Understanding the `print()` Function

The `print()` function is fundamental in Python, serving as the primary method for outputting data to the console. It's how you can communicate results or messages from your code. Whether you're outputting strings, numbers, or results of calculations, `print()` is your go-to:

```
print("Hello, World!")   # Displays a string
print(2 + 3)             # Calculates and displays the sum, showing '5'
```

## Using Escape Characters

To enhance the format of your output, Python provides escape characters:

```
print("Hello World!\n\tThis is an example of a newline and a tab.")
```

This script demonstrates \n for a new line and \t for a tab, organizing output as:

```
Hello World!
    This is an example of a newline and a tab.
```

## Common Escape Sequences Include:

| Escape Sequence | Description |
|:---:|---|
| \' | **Single Quote** - Displays a single quote inside single-quoted strings. |
| \" | **Double Quote** - Displays a double quote inside double-quoted strings. |
| \\ | **Backslash** - Displays a backslash. |
| \b | **Backspace** - Moves the cursor back one space. |
| \n | **Newline** - Moves to the next line. |

This overview introduces you to scripting with Python, from writing simple messages to controlling how text is formatted and displayed. Dive in, experiment, and start crafting your own scripts!

## 1.9 Executing a Script

Now that you're familiar with what scripts are and have been introduced to the print() function, it's time to write and execute your first Python script. Open your chosen text editor or IDE, and let's create a new file. Name it something simple like hello.py—the .py extension tells your computer that this is a Python script.

In this file, type the following line:

```
print("Hello, World!")
```

Save your file. Now, navigate to your terminal or command prompt, ensuring you're in the same directory as your hello.py file. Type python hello.py and press enter. If everything's set up correctly, you should see `Hello, World!` printed out on the screen. Congratulations, you've just written and executed your first Python script!

From writing code in a text editor to seeing it run in your terminal, this process is the backbone of Python programming. It might seem like a small step, but it's a giant leap in your coding adventure. Every complex program, application, or system starts with simple lines of code like these.

## 1.10 Taking User Input

Python makes it simple to prompt the user for input and store that input in a variable for further use. The `input()` function pauses your program and waits for the user to type something into the console, then press enter.

Let's create a script that asks for the user's name and then greets them. Open your text editor or IDE and create a new file named `greet.py`. Type in the following lines:

```
user_name = input("What is your name? ")
print("Hello, " + user_name + "!")
```

In the first line, we use the `input()` function with a string argument. This string is displayed to the user as a prompt: `"What is your name?"`. Whatever the user types in response to this prompt is then stored in the variable `user_name`.

## 1.11 Displaying Output

The second line of the script constructs a greeting message by concatenating strings and the user's input, then displays this message using the `print()` function. Here, we're using the `+` operator to concatenate, or combine, the strings "Hello, ", the user's input stored in `user_name`, and "!" into a single string that `print()` then displays.

## 1.12 Chapter Summary

As we wrap up Chapter 1, you've taken some monumental first steps on your Python programming journey. You've laid the groundwork by understanding the Python interpreter and the role of an IDE, setting up your programming environment, and executing your very first Python script. These foundational skills are your stepping stones into the vast world of programming with Python.

By installing Python and configuring your IDE, you've essentially prepared your canvas, ready to paint with the broad strokes of Python's syntax and functionalities. The simple yet iconic

`"Hello, World!"` program marks not just the beginning of many programmers' journeys but a gateway to endless possibilities that Python programming offers.

# Chapter 2: The Foundations of Python

Imagine you're about to build a house. Before you can start with the walls or the roof, you need a solid foundation. Python's foundation is built with variables, data types, and control structures. These essential elements allow you to store and manipulate data, format your output, and make decisions within your programs. Just as a house without a strong foundation is prone to collapse, your Python projects will struggle without a good grasp of these basics. Let's roll up our sleeves and start laying down the first bricks of your Python knowledge, ensuring that everything we build on top is solid and secure.

## 2.1 Variables and Data Types: The Building Blocks

Now, let's dive into the nitty-gritty of variables and data types, the building blocks that will help you structure and store data in your Python endeavors. Think of this as laying the foundation for your Python house. Without a strong foundation, everything you try to build on top will have difficulty standing.

### Declaration and Assignment

In Python, creating a variable is as straightforward as telling a friend your name. You simply assign a value to a name, and voilà, you've declared a variable. Python uses a dynamic typing

# Chapter 2: The Foundations of Python

system, meaning you don't have to state the type of data your variable represents explicitly; Python figures it out based on the value you assign.

Here's a quick example:

```
my_favorite_number = 26
```

In this line, `my_favorite_number` is now a variable that holds the value `26`. You've just told Python, "Hey, whenever I say `my_favorite_number`, I'm referring to `26`."

*Side note: This is a "factual" program. 26 is my favorite number because, at the age of 26, you get the biggest price break in car insurance rates (in the US). Then it's just aches and pains from there!*

## Primitive

Data types are essentially categories for your data. Python organizes data into types such as integers, floats, strings, and booleans.

- **Integers** are whole numbers, positive or negative, without a decimal point. For example, `10` or `-3`.
- **Floats** are floating-point numbers, which means they have a decimal point. Like `0.001` or `10.7` or to store π (Pi) `3.1415926535`
- **Strings** are sequences of characters used for text. They're wrapped in quotes like `"hello"` or `'Python is fun!'`.
- **Booleans** represent truth values and can be either `True` or `False`.

Other data types include lists, dictionaries, sets, and bytes, which we will cover in detail later in this book.

## Type Conversion

Sometimes, you need to transform data from one type to another, like changing a string into an integer to perform arithmetic. This is known as type conversion or casting. Python provides built-in functions for this purpose: `int()`, `float()`, and `str()`, among others.

Imagine you're building a simple app that asks for a user's age and then calculates how old they'll be in five years. The user input comes as a string, so you'll need to convert that input into an integer before doing the math:

```
age_now = input("How old are you? ")
age_in_five_years = int(age_now) + 5
print(f"In five years, you'll be {age_in_five_years} years old.")
```

By understanding and utilizing type conversion, you ensure your data is in the right format for the task at hand.

The last line introduced F-String without explanation. F-String and the format() method are slick ways to format output. Let's talk about them next.

## 2.2 Rules for Naming Variables

When working with variables in Python, it's essential to follow a set of rules for naming them, known as identifier rules. These rules ensure that your code is valid, readable, and maintainable. Let's explore these rules:

### Start with a Letter or an Underscore

A variable name must begin with a letter (a-z, A-Z) or an underscore (_). It cannot start with a digit. This is because Python needs to distinguish between variables and numbers.

```
valid_variable = 10
_valid_variable = 20
```

Invalid Examples:

```
1st_variable = 30   # Starts with a digit (Invalid)
```

### Use Letters, Digits, and Underscores

After the first character, a variable name can include letters, digits, and underscores. Python allows a wide range of names, but choosing meaningful ones is essential.

```
user_name = "Alice"
user1 = "Bob"
user_name_2 = "Charlie"
```

Invalid Examples:

```
user-name = "Alice"   # Hyphens are not allowed (Invalid)
user name = "Bob"     # Spaces are not allowed (Invalid)
```

## Case Sensitivity

Python treats variable names as case-sensitive. This means that Variable, variable, and VARIABLE are considered three different identifiers.

```
Variable = 100
variable = 200
VARIABLE = 300
```

These are distinct variables, so consider case sensitivity when naming and using variables in your programs.

## Avoid Python Keywords

Python has a set of reserved words known as keywords, which have special meanings in the language. These cannot be used as variable names. Examples include if, else, while, for, class, and def.

```
# Invalid Example:
class = "Advanced Python"   # 'class' is a reserved keyword (Invalid)
```

To check the list of keywords in your Python version, you can use the following code:

```
import keyword
print(keyword.kwlist)
```

## Use Non-English Characters with Care

Python is flexible—it allows you to use characters from other languages in your variable names. This means you can write code using Spanish, Hindi, or even symbols like π.

For example:

```
año_de_nacimiento = 1995   # Spanish for 'year of birth'
नाम = "अर्जुन"              # Hindi for 'name'
π = 3.1415926535
```

This feature can be helpful in personal projects, educational settings, or when working primarily with others who speak your native language. It can make your code feel more intuitive and accessible at first.

However, it's important to know that in professional programming, it's considered best practice to use English-based identifiers. Here's why:

- Most programming languages, libraries, and documentation use English

- English identifiers are easier to understand in international teams
- English-based code is easier to share, maintain, and contribute to

You don't need to speak English fluently to succeed as a programmer. Many developers worldwide learn just enough English to read and write code—and still go on to build amazing things.

So, while Python lets you use your native language in code, this book follows the global standard of using English-based variables and function names. It's part of teaching best practices from the start—and setting you up for success.

## Anti–"War and Peace" Identifiers (Keep It Descriptive but Concise)

While Python allows lengthy variable names, it's best to keep them **concise yet descriptive enough** to clearly convey the variable's purpose. This practice improves code readability and makes your life easier down the road.

Python won't stop you from writing something like:

```
total_amount_to_be_paid_after_applying_all_possible_discounts_and_credits = 250.75
```

…but that doesn't mean you should.

At one company, we jokingly called these "War and Peace" identifiers—a reference to the famously 1,400-page novel by Leo Tolstoy—dense, dramatic, and full of characters (nearly 600 of them). These names were so long, you practically needed a bookmark and a couple of coffee breaks to finish reading them.

```
total_due = 250.75
final_amount = 250.75
total_with_discounts = 250.75
```

These are still meaningful, but far more readable and easier to maintain.

And of course, names that are too short—like tp—aren't much better. The goal is to find the sweet spot: a name that's clear and useful, but not a burden to type. A good variable name tells a story—but it shouldn't feel like reading a novel.

## Use Underscores for Readability

For multi-word variable names, Python uses underscores to separate words. This style is called **snake_case**, and it's the convention recommended by Python's official PEP 8 style guide.

```
# Good Example:
first_name = "John"

# Less Readable Example:
firstname = "John"
```

You may have seen other styles like camelCase or PascalCase in other languages like JavaScript or Java. In Python, we stick with snake_case for variable and function names—not because it's objectively better, but because it's the community standard. **And in programming, consistency is one of the most important best practices,** of any language. Following this convention makes your code more readable to other Python programmers and aligns with best practices.

By following these rules, you'll write Python code that's not only valid but also clear and easy to maintain. Whether you're using English, Hindi, Spanish, or even mathematical symbols like π, properly named variables make your programs easier to read, understand, and debug, which is a crucial part of becoming an effective programmer.

## 2.3 String Formatting in Python: F-Strings and `format()` Method

Python offers several ways to format strings, making integrating variables and expressions within text easier. Two popular methods are f-strings, introduced in Python 3.6, and the `format()` method.

### F-Strings

F-strings, or formatted string literals, allow for the direct inclusion of expressions inside string literals using curly braces { }. These expressions are evaluated at runtime, which simplifies the process of string formatting:

```
age_in_five_years = 25
print(f"In five years, you'll be {age_in_five_years} years old.")
# Output: In five years, you'll be 25 years old.
```

F-strings excel in formatting floats by including a colon : followed by a format specifier inside the curly braces, enabling precise control over numerical displays:

```
temperature = 23.45678
print(f"The current temperature is {temperature:.2f}°C.")
# Output: The current temperature is 23.46°C.
```

In this example, with `{temperature:.2f}` we are instructing Python to display a float value found in `temperature`, with 2 decimal places. Notice that it also rounded up.

## The `format()` Method

Before f-strings were introduced, the `format()` method was commonly used for string formatting. It replaces placeholders defined by curly braces { } with values specified in the method call:

```
name = "Sophia"
age = 30
print("Hello, {0}. You are {1} years old.".format(name, age))
# Output: Hello, Sophia. You are 30 years old.
```

The `format()` method is versatile and supports various formatting options, including positional and keyword arguments:

- **Positional Arguments**: The numbers inside the curly braces refer to the position of the arguments provided in the `format()` method.
- **Keyword Arguments**: Named placeholders can also be used, making the code more readable:

```
print("Hello, {name}. You are {age} years old.".format(name="Sophia", age=30))
# Output: Hello, Sophia. You are 30 years old.
```

- **Floating-Point Formatting**: The `{:.2f}` format specifier is used to format floating-point numbers to two decimal places:

```
temperature = 23.45678
print("The current temperature is {:.2f}°C.".format(temperature))
# Output: The current temperature is 23.46°C.
```

Here, the temperature variable is formatted to show only two decimal places (23.46), and the number is rounded to the nearest value.

**More Examples of Formatting with format()**

1. **Aligning Text**: You can align text using < (left), > (right), or ^ (center) within a specified width:

```
print("Left aligned:   |{:<10}|".format("apple"))
# Output: Left aligned:   |apple     |

print("Right aligned:  |{:>10}|".format("apple"))
# Output: Right aligned:  |     apple|

print("Center aligned:|{:^10}|".format("apple"))
```

## Chapter 2: The Foundations of Python

```
# Output: Center aligned:|   apple    |
```

2. **Formatting Numbers with Commas**: Adding commas for thousands separators:

```
number = 1234567
print("Number with commas: {:,}".format(number))
# Output: Number with commas: 1,234,567
```

**NERD NOTES** *Commas, Periods, and Culture Clashes*

*Most readers never think about number formatting... until they see a ",", where a "." should be—and then chaos ensues.*

*By default, Python formats numbers using U.S. conventions: commas for thousands and periods for decimals. If your country does the reverse—like 1.234,56 instead of 1,234.56—that can be confusing.*

*Good news: Python lets you format numbers **your way** using the locale module:*

```
import locale
locale.setlocale(locale.LC_ALL, 'es_MX.UTF-8')   # Use your region's code
number = 1234567
print("Localized: {:n}".format(number))
# Output: 1.234.567
```

🍷 *Tip: If you get an error, try* `locale.setlocale(locale.LC_ALL, '')` *to use your system's default settings. On macOS or Linux, run* `locale -a` *in the terminal to see available options.*

3. **Formatting Numbers with Commas and Decimal Places**: Formatting a number with both commas and two decimal places:

```
number = 12345.674
print("Number with commas and two decimal places: {:,.2f}".format(number))
# Output: Number with commas and two decimal places: 12,345.67
```

4. **Padding Numbers with Zeros**: You can pad numbers with zeros to ensure they have a certain width:

```
print("Padded with zeros: {:05d}".format(42))
# Output: Padded with zeros: 00042
```

## Choosing Between F-Strings and `format()`

Choosing between f-strings and the `.format()` method often comes down to personal preference or specific project requirements. Both are valid options, but here are some factors to consider:

- **Readability and Conciseness:** F-strings generally offer a more concise and intuitive syntax, making them a popular choice for many developers.
- **Compatibility:** The `.format()` method is valuable for projects that need to support older Python versions.
- **Dynamic Formatting:** In scenarios where the format string itself needs to be constructed dynamically, the `.format()` method might be more suitable due to its clear separation of the format template from the data being inserted.

## Debugging

Both f-strings and the `format()` method can be used effectively for debugging. F-strings have the advantage of the `=` specifier, which simplifies debugging by automatically including both variable names and their values:

```
count = 10
print(f"{count=}")        # Output: count=10
```

Whether you choose f-strings for their simplicity and readability or the `format()` method for its flexibility and compatibility, Python's string formatting capabilities greatly enhance code clarity and maintainability. Understanding how and when to use these tools is essential for effective Python programming.

# 2.4 Understanding Immutability

Some data types in Python are immutable, meaning that once they're created, their content cannot be changed. Strings are a classic example of an immutable type. When you think you're modifying a string, you're creating a new string with the changes.

This might sound like a quirk, but it's by design. Immutability has several benefits, including easier debugging and optimization by Python under the hood. Here's a quick illustration:

```
original_string = "cat"
modified_string = original_string + "s"
```

What happens here is that the `original_string` does not get an "s" added to it. Instead, `modified_string` is a totally new string that combines `original_string` and "s". Understanding this behavior is key, especially as you start to manipulate data more complexly.

Variables and data types are the alphabet of Python's language. Mastery of these basics sets a solid foundation for your coding projects, allowing you to communicate with your computer effectively and write programs that solve real-world problems. As you become more comfortable with these concepts, you'll find that they're the stepping stones to understanding more complex Python features and functionalities.

## 2.5 Comments: Your Code's Annotation

As we transition from understanding Python's building blocks to making decisions in our code with control structures, let's take a moment to discuss a key aspect of writing clean, understandable code: comments.

Comments are like notes to yourself and others who will read your code, explaining what the code does and why certain decisions were made. Python supports single-line comments, initiated with a # symbol, and multi-line comments, which can be created using triple quotes ( ' ' ' or """).

```
# This is a single-line comment

"""
this is a multiple-line
comment
"""
```

As we delve into more complex concepts, such as control structures, the ability to annotate your code with comments becomes invaluable. It helps you keep track of your thought process and makes your code more accessible to others.

### Best Practices for Python Comments

1. **Clarity Over Quantity**: Write comments that clarify complex parts of your code; avoid stating the obvious. Good comments explain the "why" behind a code block, not just the "what."

2. **Stay Up-to-Date**: Ensure comments and the code they describe are updated. Outdated comments can be more misleading than no comments at all.

3. **Avoid Redundant Comments**: Do not repeat what is already obvious from the code. For instance, avoid comments like `x = x + 1  # Increment x`.

4. **Use Inline Comments Sparingly**: Inline comments are placed on the same line as a statement. They should be used sparingly and only when they significantly add to the understanding of the code.

```
total = sum(values)   # Sum values in a list
```

5. **Keep Comments Near Their Relevant Code**: Place comments close to the part of the code they explain. This makes it easier for the reader to understand the comment's context without jumping around the file.

6. **Comment on Blocks of Code If Necessary**: When several lines of code work together to achieve a purpose, consider adding a comment at the beginning of the block to explain its overall function.

7. **Explain Complex Algorithms or Decisions**: If your code uses a complex algorithm or if there is a specific reason for making a non-obvious decision, document it.

8. **Use TODOs to Mark Improvements**: Use TODO comments to mark places where improvements could be made or additional features could be implemented in the future.

```
# TODO: Optimize this function for larger datasets
```

For the longest time, the software world pushed loading your code with comments: "Comments are awesome; put them everywhere." But what we have found is that comments become stale, meaning that the code gets updated, but the comments don't. This does cause lots of confusion, which can introduce bugs in the code.

There is a powerful concept called "self-documenting code." This concept states that code is written in such a clear manner that it becomes obvious what it is doing. This concept is used with comments; it doesn't replace them.

Much of the code in this book will be "overly" commented on to help you understand what it is doing. Typically, this isn't the norm in production code. For now, document away to help you learn. Later, in the appendix, we will talk about self-documenting code and how to apply it.

## 2.6 Control Structures: Making Decisions in Your Code

Picture yourself at a crossroads in an enchanting forest, where each path leads to a different adventure. In your Python code, you often need to make decisions based on data or calculations that will change your code's path. This is where control structures come into play, acting as the decision-making heart of your code. They help your program decide which operations to perform based on certain conditions, making your code smarter and more dynamic.

 ### The Earth is Flat - Conditional Statements

Let's take an example from the official Python documentation (*using the Python Interpreter, 2025 [https://docs.python.org/3/tutorial/interpreter.html]*) that demonstrates a simple use of a boolean variable and an `if` statement:

```
the_earth_is_flat = True
if the_earth_is_flat:
    print("Be careful not to fall off!")
```

Since `the_earth_is_flat` is true, it will output `Be careful not to fall off!`

*I don't subscribe to the belief that the Earth is flat. But if I happen to be wrong, this program provides an important safety tip.*

You may look at this code and think, "That's easy. I get it!" But in the next section, let's point out a couple of important things you might not have caught.

## 2.7 Understanding Python Syntax: Indentation and the Colon

Syntax in any programming language is like grammar in a spoken language; it's a set of rules that governs how words and phrases are put together to form meaningful sentences. In Python, syntax plays a crucial role in the structure and execution of code. Two fundamental aspects of Python syntax that beginners must understand are **indentation** and the use of the **colon (:)**.

### Indentation Matters

In Python, whitespace is not just for readability; it's a part of the syntax. Indentation indicates a block of code that belongs together. Unlike many other programming languages that use braces {} to define a block of code, Python uses indentation levels. This means that all the code aligned at the same level of indentation is considered to be part of the same block.

```
# Correct Indentation
if the_earth_is_flat:
    print("Be careful not to fall off!")   # This line belongs to the if block

# Incorrect Indentation
if the_earth_is_flat:
print("Be careful not to fall off!")   # IndentationError: expected an indented block
```

## Syntax Errors and Best Practices

Not adhering to syntax rules results in syntax errors. To avoid these errors:

- Use four spaces per indentation level, as per PEP 8, Python's style guide.
- Do not mix tabs and spaces, as this can lead to confusing errors.
- Use an IDE or text editor that shows whitespace characters and is configured to insert spaces when the Tab key is pressed.

> **NERD NOTES** *PEP 8: Because Ugly Code is a Crime*
>
> **What is PEP 8?** *It is Python's official style guide, essential for writing clean, readable code. It details how to format Python code, emphasizing readability and consistency across the Python community.*
>
> **Importance of Coding Styles:**
> - **Readability:** *Makes your code easier for others to read and understand.*
> - **Maintenance:** *Consistent style helps in maintaining and updating code efficiently.*
> - **Community Integration:** *Adhering to common standards allows for better collaboration and contribution to public projects.*
>
> **Learn More:** *The detailed discussion in the Appendix provides a deeper dive into the rules and best practices of PEP 8.*

## Practicing Syntax

The best way to become comfortable with Python's syntax is through practice. Write small scripts, use Python's interactive mode, or utilize online interpreters to get immediate feedback on your syntax usage. Paying attention to syntax details from the beginning will make you a more effective programmer and prevent common errors as you learn.

By understanding and adhering to Python's syntax rules, you ensure that your code is not only correct but also readable and maintainable. As you continue to learn Python, these syntax foundations will become second nature, allowing you to focus on solving problems and writing great code.

### The Earth is Round

But in the same spirit of the Earth being flat, I'm proposing a second theory, which is that the Earth is round. And if I'm right, then let's explore a more "down to earth" version of our program that calculates the surface of the Earth.

```
the_earth_is_flat = False
the_earth_is_donut_shaped = False

if the_earth_is_flat:
    print("Be careful not to fall off!")
elif the_earth_is_donut_shaped:
    print("Hmmm, interesting theory.")
    print("Not sure how to calculate that.")
else:
    PI = 3.14159265359
    RADIUS_IN_MI = 3959
    RADIUS_IN_KM = 6371
    earth_area_in_mi = 4 * PI * (RADIUS_IN_MI ** 2)
    earth_area_in_km = 4 * PI * (RADIUS_IN_KM ** 2)
    print("The surface area of the Earth:")
    print(f"in square miles is {earth_area_in_mi}")
    print(f"and in square kilometers is {earth_area_in_km}")
```

## 2.8 Constants

You may be wondering why some of these variables are in uppercase. In Python, it is a common convention to write constants in all caps. **Constants** are values that are meant to remain unchanged throughout the program. By writing them in uppercase, we signal to anyone reading the code that these values should not be modified.

For example, in our code:

```
PI = 3.14159265359
RADIUS_IN_MI = 3959
RADIUS_IN_KM = 6371
```

These are constants because their values do not change during the execution of the program. The value of `PI` represents the mathematical constant, while `RADIUS_IN_MI` and `RADIUS_IN_KM` represent the Earth's radius in miles and kilometers, respectively—fixed values used in our calculations.

On the other hand, `earth_area_in_mi` and `earth_area_in_km` are lowercase because they are variables whose values are calculated dynamically based on the formula. They depend on the constant values but are not themselves constants, as their values are derived and could change if we modify the formula or input values.

Using all caps for constants improves code readability and helps avoid accidental modification of values that are not meant to change. While Python doesn't enforce immutability of constants (like `final` in Java or `const` in C++), following this convention is considered good practice in Python programming.

## 2.9 `if`, `elif`, and `else`

This is a classic example where `if`, `elif`, and `else` statements shine. These statements evaluate whether a condition is true or false, leading to actions based on those checks.

The `elif` statement is a seamless blend of `else` and `if`, enabling a conditional check right after an initial `if` condition is found to be false, before potentially defaulting to an `else` block. The same thing could be accomplished by doing something like this:

```python
if the_earth_is_flat:
    print("Be careful not to fall off!")
elseif the_earth_is_donut_shaped:
    print("Hmmm, interesting theory.")
    print("Not sure how to calculate that.")
else:
    ...
```

## 2.10 Calculations in Python

In our "science project," we use $4\pi R^2$ to calculate the surface of the Earth. This is how to code it in Python:

```python
earth_area_in_mi = 4 * PI * (RADIUS_IN_MI ** 2)
earth_area_in_km = 4 * PI * (RADIUS_IN_KM ** 2)
```

`PI`, `RADIUS_IN_MI`, and `RADIUS_IN_KM` are all constants defined right after the `else`. In Python speak, `*` represents multiply, and `**` is the exponentiation operator. So, `r ** 2` means "r squared" or $R^2$

The output of this version of the program is:

```
The surface area of the Earth:
in square miles is 196961284.33725268
and in square kilometers is 510064471.90982187
```

CHAPTER 2: THE FOUNDATIONS OF PYTHON

 **NERD NOTES** *You Might Be a Nerd If...*

*Now, should you feel the impulse to point out that the Earth's radius varies between the equator and the poles, then you've rightfully earned your 'nerd' badge.*

*If this thought hasn't crossed your mind, fret not; there will be plenty more chances for you to demonstrate your nerdiness.*

## 2.11 Python Operators

Operators in Python can be broadly categorized into three main types: logical operators, comparison operators, and arithmetic operators. Each category serves a distinct purpose, enabling programmers to express conditions, compare values, and perform mathematical computations efficiently and precisely.

### Arithmetic Operators

Arithmetic operators perform calculations. In our "Earth is Round Science Project", we used two arithmetic operators, * and **, but there are others:

| Operator | Description |
|---|---|
| + | Addition - Adds values on either side of the operator. |
| - | Subtraction - Subtracts the right-hand operand from the left-hand operand. |
| * | Multiplies values on either side of the operator. |
| / | Divides the left-hand operand by the right-hand operand. |
| // | Floor Division – Divides the left-hand number by the right-hand number and rounds the result down to the nearest whole number. For example, 7 // 2 equals 3 (not 3.5, because it rounds down). |
| % | Divides the left-hand operand by the right-hand operand and returns the remainder. |
| ** | Performs exponential (power) calculation on operators. |

### Understanding Arithmetic Operator Precedence

In Python, as in mathematics, different operations are not all created equally. Some take priority over others. This hierarchy determines the order in which operations are evaluated in complex expressions. This concept is known as "operator precedence."

## Why Operator Precedence Matters

Consider the expression 3 + 4 * 5. Is it evaluated as (3 + 4) * 5 or 3 + (4 * 5)? Arithmetic operator precedence answers this question. In Python, multiplication has a higher precedence than addition, so the correct evaluation is 3 + (4 * 5), yielding 23 rather than 35.

## The Order of Arithmetic Operations

Python follows a specific order of arithmetic operations, often remembered by the acronym PEMDAS, which stands for:

- Parentheses
- Exponents
- Multiplication and Division
- Addition and Subtraction

Within each category, operations are performed from left to right. However, it's important to note that multiplication and division are of equal precedence; the same goes for addition and subtraction.

## Table of Arithmetic Operator Precedence

Below is a simplified table showing the precedence of arithmetic operators in Python, from highest to lowest:

| Operand(s) | Description |
| --- | --- |
| () | Used to override the default precedence. |
| ** | Exponents |
| * / // % | Multiplication, Division, Floor Division, and Modulus all have the same level of precedence. |
| + - | Addition and Subtraction |

**NERD NOTES** *Sacred Order of Operations*

*For the math nerds among us, rejoice! You'll notice that Python respects the sacred hierarchy of arithmetic operators' precedence, ensuring your numerical wizardry behaves as expected.*

## Best Practices

- **Use Parentheses**: When in doubt, use parentheses to clarify the order of operations. Not only does this ensure that the expression is evaluated as intended, but it also increases readability for anyone else reading your code.
- **Avoid Complex Expressions**: Break down complex expressions into smaller parts. This can prevent errors caused by misunderstanding arithmetic operator precedence and make your code easier to read and maintain.
- **Consistency**: Be consistent in how you structure expressions. Consistency helps prevent errors and makes your intentions clear to others.

## Example Expression

Let's dive into an example to understand how Python evaluates expressions. Consider the expression: `4 + 3 * 2 ** 2 - 1`

1. **Exponents**: `2 ** 2` is evaluated first, becoming `4`.
2. **Multiplication**: `3 * 4` is next, simplifying to `12`.
3. **Addition and Subtraction**: Finally, we perform the addition and subtraction from left to right, `4 + 12 - 1`, resulting in `15`.

Understanding arithmetic operator precedence allows you to correctly write expressions that the Python interpreter understands and helps you debug code when you get unexpected results.

## Comparison Operators

Imagine you're designing a high-score tracker for a video game. The game needs to determine if a player's current score surpasses the high score to update it and celebrate the achievement. This is where comparison operators shine, enabling us to compare values within our code. Let's dive into an example that incorporates these operators:

```
current_score = 450
high_score = 400

if current_score > high_score:
    print("Congratulations! You've set a new high score.")
    high_score = current_score
else:
    print("Keep trying to beat the high score!")
```

In this snippet, the > is a comparison operator that checks if `current_score` is greater than `high_score`. If the condition is true, the program congratulates the player and updates the `high_score` variable to the new score. Otherwise, it encourages the player to keep trying.

Comparison operators are fundamental in evaluating conditions. They allow our programs to make decisions and respond differently based on the inputs, creating dynamic and interactive experiences. By skillfully applying these operators, we can craft logical conditions that guide the flow of our programs, making them more intuitive and responsive to the user.

Python has quite a few comparison operators. Here is a list:

| Operand | Description |
| --- | --- |
| == | Check if the value of two operands is equal; if yes, the condition becomes true. |
| != | Check if the values of two operands are equal or not; if the values are not equal, then the condition becomes true. |
| > | It checks if the value of the left operand is greater than the value of the right operand; if yes, then the condition becomes true. |
| < | It checks if the value of the left operand is less than the value of the right operand; if yes, then the condition becomes true. |
| >= | It checks if the value of the left operand is greater than or equal to the value of the right operand. If yes, then the condition becomes true. |
| <= | It checks if the value of the left operand is less than or equal to the value of the right operand. If yes, then the condition becomes true. |

## Logical Operators

Let's say that we want the heating to turn on not just based on temperature but also if it's nighttime. This scenario calls for logical operators `and`, `or`, `not`, introducing complexity into our conditions. These operators allow you to combine multiple conditions into a single if statement, making your decision-making process even more powerful. Using the earlier example, but with an additional condition for night-time:

```
temperature = 18
is_night = True
if temperature < 20 and is_night:
    print("It's cold and night. Turning the heating on.")
else:
    print("No need for heating right now.")
```

Here, both conditions must be true (it must be cold `and` night) for the system to decide to turn the heating on. Logical operators are invaluable for crafting more nuanced, intelligent decision flows in your programs.

These are Python's logical operators:

| Operand | Description |
|---|---|
| and | Logical AND - If both the operands are true, then the condition becomes true. |
| or | Logical OR - If any of the two operands are true, then the condition becomes true. |
| not | Logical NOT - Used to reverse the logical state of its operand. |

## Best Practices

When it comes to writing conditional statements, clarity is king. Here are a few best practices to keep your code clean and understandable:

- **Use Clear Variable Names**: Variables like `is_night` instantly tell you what they represent, making your conditions easier to read.
- **Avoid Deep Nesting**: Deeply nested `if` statements (that is, inside if statements, inside if statements, etc.) can make your code hard to follow. Try to simplify complex conditions or break them into smaller functions.
- **Be Explicit in Conditions**: Instead of writing `if is_night == True:`, you can simply write `if is_night:`. However, being explicit, like using `is not None` when checking for `None`, can make your intentions clearer.

Implementing these practices helps keep your code readable and maintainable, ensuring that others (and you in the future) can easily understand your program's decisions.

## 2.12 Ternary Conditional Expression

Imagine you're planning your outfit for the day based on the weather. You might think, "If it's raining, I'll wear boots; otherwise, I'll wear sneakers." In code, it looks like this:

```
if weather == "raining":
    outfit = "boots"
else:
    outfit = "sneakers"
```

This decision-making process can be mapped to a ternary operator in Python:

```
outfit = "boots" if weather == "raining" else "sneakers"
```

A ternary conditional expression consists of three parts: the "true" part, the "condition," and the "false" part. Here's how it breaks down:

$$\text{outfit} = \underbrace{\text{"boots"}}_{\text{true}} \underbrace{\text{if weather == "raining"}}_{\text{condition}} \underbrace{\text{else "sneakers"}}_{\text{false}}$$

This means, set the `outfit` variable to "boots" if `weather` equals "raining"; otherwise, set it to "sneakers." Simple, right?

Here's another example. Suppose you want to display a message about outstanding invoices:

```
invoice_count = 2
print(f"You have {invoice_count} outstanding invoices")
```

But if you have only one invoice, the message would be incorrect grammatically. Using a ternary expression:

```
invoice_count = 1
print(f"You have {invoice_count} outstanding invoice{'s' if invoice_count != 1 else ''}")
```

## Why Use Ternary Conditional Expressions?

- Conciseness: Condenses multiple lines of an if-else block into a single line.
- Readability: Clear and readable for simple conditions.
- Efficiency: Quickly evaluate and assign a value based on a condition.

## Caution with Nested Ternary Expressions

Avoid nesting ternary expressions to maintain readability and ease of debugging. For complex conditions, use traditional if-else statements:

```
if a > b:
    result = "Condition A"
elif b > c:
    result = "Condition B"
else:
    result = "Condition C"
```

# 2.13 Chapter Summary

This chapter covers a lot, but it also lays the groundwork essential for any aspiring Python programmer.

Chapter 2: The Foundations of Python

This chapter equipped you with the fundamental concepts of variables, data types, and basic control structures. These are the building blocks upon which all Python programs are built, enabling you to store, manipulate, and make decisions with data efficiently. By grasping these concepts, you're now prepared to dive deeper into the world of Python programming, ready to tackle more sophisticated challenges with confidence.

Looking ahead to Chapter 3, we'll shift our focus from the individual elements of Python to the art of organizing and structuring your data more effectively. Our attention turns to Python's powerful data structures—`lists`, `dictionaries`, and `sets`. These tools are invaluable for managing and accessing data in a logical and efficient way, further broadening your programming toolkit. As you become more adept at using these structures, you'll find they open up new possibilities for solving complex problems and making your code cleaner and more expressive. Let's continue our journey into Python, where structuring data smartly is the next step toward mastering this versatile language.

---

## 2.14 Suggested Exercises

Try the following exercises to reinforce your understanding of the concepts covered in this chapter. Each exercise is designed to help you practice different aspects of Python programming. You can find the solutions to each of the exercises in Appendix A at the back of the book.

### Exercise 1: Basic Variable Assignment

**Description**: In this exercise, you will practice assigning values to variables of different data types and printing them. This will help you understand how to work with integers, floats, strings, and booleans in Python.

**Task**: Assign values to variables of different data types (integer, float, string, boolean) and print them.

### Exercise 2: Type Conversion

**Description**: This exercise focuses on type conversion, which is converting one data type to another. You will write a script that takes a user input (string), converts it to an integer, performs a calculation, and then prints the result.

**Task**: Write a script that takes a user input (string), converts it to an integer, performs a calculation, and then prints the result.

## Exercise 3: String Formatting

**Description**: Learn how to format strings using f-strings and the `format()` method. This exercise will help you create strings that include variable values and format them to display properly.

**Task**: Create a string using both f-strings and the `format()` method that includes a variable integer and float, displaying them to two decimal places.

## Exercise 4: Control Structures

**Description**: Practice using control structures to make decisions in your code. In this exercise, you will write a script that asks the user for a number and checks if the number is positive, negative, or zero, printing an appropriate message for each case.

**Task**: Write a script that asks the user for a number and checks if the number is positive, negative, or zero, printing an appropriate message for each case.

## Exercise 5: Arithmetic Operations

**Description**: Get hands-on with Python's arithmetic operators by performing various calculations. This exercise will help you understand how to use operators like addition, subtraction, multiplication, division, and exponentiation.

**Task**: Write a script that performs and prints the results of addition, subtraction, multiplication, division, and exponentiation of two numbers provided by the user.

## Exercise 6: Comparison and Logical Operators

**Description**: Explore Python's comparison and logical operators by creating a script that categorizes a user's age. This exercise will enhance your understanding of how to compare values and combine conditions.

**Task**: Create a script that asks the user for their age and determines if they are a child, teenager, adult, or senior, using both comparison and logical operators.

## Exercise 7: Ternary Conditional Expression

**Description**: Learn to use ternary conditional expressions for concise decision-making in your code. This exercise involves writing a script that uses a ternary expression to determine whether a user's input number is even or odd.

**Task**: Write a script that determines whether a user's input number is even or odd using a ternary conditional expression.

---

# 2.15 Project: Loan Payment Calculator

Are you ready to tackle your first project? I think so.

Like all projects in this book, you can download the final solution from GitHub. For more details, refer to the Appendix.

**Objective**: Enhance your understanding of Python by developing a Loan Payment Calculator that accounts for optional down payments and handles a 0% interest rate. This project will deepen your knowledge of variables, data types, and arithmetic operations and introduce you to making decisions in your code using conditional logic.

## Step-by-Step Guide:

1. **Prompt for Basic Loan Information**:
   - Ask the user to input the total loan amount for the car.
   - Request the annual interest rate as a percentage. The user should be able to input a number like 7.5 for a 7.5% rate.
   - Inquire about the loan duration in years from the user.
2. **Inquire About Down Payment**:
   - Ask the user if they want to include a down payment.
   - If the user answers yes, prompt for the down payment amount and adjust the loan amount accordingly by subtracting the down payment from the initial loan amount.
3. **Calculate Monthly Payment**:
   - First, check if the annual interest rate is greater than 0.
     - If yes, convert the annual interest rate to a monthly rate and proceed with the regular loan payment calculation formula.
     - If the interest rate is 0%, calculate the monthly payment by simply dividing the loan amount (after adjusting for any down payment) by the total number of payments (loan duration in years multiplied by 12).
   - Use the formula to calculate the monthly payment of a loan. The formula is:

$$M = \frac{P \times r}{1 - (1+r)^{-n}}$$

where:

- M is the monthly payment.
- P is the loan amount (principal).
- r is the monthly interest rate (annual interest rate divided by 12).
- n is the total number of payments (loan duration in years multiplied by 12).

The point of this project is not to know how to read math formulas, so here is the code to calculate the monthly payment:

```
# Car loan monthly payment calculation
numerator = loan_amount * monthly_interest_rate
denominator = 1 - (1 + monthly_interest_rate) ** -total_payments
monthly_payment = numerator / denominator
```

4. **Output Detailed Loan Information**:
    - Display the loan amount (after any down payment adjustment).
    - Show the total number of payments and the duration of the loan in years.
    - Present the interest rate to the user.
    - Finally, display the calculated monthly payment, formatted to two decimal places.

## Tips for Success:

- **Clarity and Precision**: Ensure your prompts are clear so the user knows exactly what information to enter. Precision in instructions leads to accurate inputs.
- **Variable Naming**: Use descriptive names for your variables to make your code self-explanatory and easier to follow.
- **Implement Conditional Logic**: Use `if` statements effectively to guide the program's flow based on the user's inputs about the down payment and interest rate.
- **Test Thoroughly**: Run your program with different scenarios (including with and without a down payment, with a 0% and a positive interest rate) to ensure it behaves as expected under various conditions.

By completing this project, you'll not only practice basic Python programming concepts but also learn how to incorporate conditional logic to make your programs more dynamic and adaptable to user input. This practical application reinforces the fundamentals and helps you build the confidence to tackle more complex coding challenges.

## Chapter 2: The Foundations of Python

## Example of Possible Output

```
Enter purchase amount: 15000
Annual interest rate: 10
Loan duration (years): 5
Include down payment? (y/n): y
Down payment amount: 2000

Loan Details:
    Purchase Amount: $15000.00
    Down Payment: $2000.00
    Loan Amount: $13000.00
    Number of Payments: 60 (5 years)
    Interest Rate: 10.000
    Monthly Payment: $276.21
```

# Chapter 3: Exploring Python with Loops and Collections

Make your kitchen a place where you have different drawers and cabinets to keep things organized. In Python, we have various data structures to help us organize and manage our data efficiently. In this chapter, we will explore some of these essential data structures, such as lists, dictionaries, tuples, and sets, as well as loops that allow us to perform repetitive tasks. Understanding these concepts will help you write more efficient and organized code.

## 3.1 Lists

Lists in Python are like those versatile kitchen drawers. You can stuff them with different items, from integers and strings to even other lists. Creating a list is as simple as enclosing items in square brackets [], separated by commas. For instance, `ingredients = ["flour", "sugar", "eggs"]` neatly packages your cake ingredients into a single, tidy variable.

Lists are one of the most versatile data types in Python. They allow you to store multiple items in a single variable. Lists are ordered and changeable, and duplicate values are allowed. Lists are essential for many real-world applications, such as storing a collection of items, maintaining a sequence of events, or holding data retrieved from databases.

CHAPTER 3: EXPLORING PYTHON WITH LOOPS AND COLLECTIONS

## Understanding List Indexing

In Python, lists are zero-indexed. This means that the first element of a list is accessed with the index 0, the second element with the index 1, and so on. This can be a bit different from how we naturally count items (starting from 1), but it is a fundamental concept in Python and many other programming languages.

Let's look at an example to clarify this:

```python
# Creating a list
fruits = ["apple", "banana", "cherry"]

# Accessing list items
print(fruits[0])  # Output: apple (1st item)
print(fruits[1])  # Output: banana (2nd item)
print(fruits[2])  # Output: cherry (3rd item)
```

In this example:

- `fruits[0]` accesses the first item, "apple".
- `fruits[1]` accesses the second item, "banana".
- `fruits[2]` accesses the third item, "cherry".

Understanding this zero-based indexing is crucial when working with lists and arrays in Python.

## List Operations

You can perform various operations on lists, such as adding, removing, and modifying elements:

```python
# Adding items to the list
fruits.append("orange")  # Adds "orange" to the end of the list
fruits.insert(1, "blueberry")  # Inserts "blueberry" at index 1

# Removing items from the list
fruits.remove("banana")  # Removes "banana" from the list
popped_fruit = fruits.pop()  # Removes and returns the last item
```

```
# Modifying list items
fruits[0] = "kiwi"   # Changes the first item to "kiwi"
```

Understanding how to create, access, and manipulate lists is fundamental in Python programming. It allows you to manage and organize data efficiently, setting the stage for more advanced concepts.

## 3.2 Understanding Multi-dimensional Arrays in Python

Multi-dimensional arrays are collections that contain other collections. They're perfect for representing complex data structures like matrices, grids, or, in our case, a bookshelf with multiple shelves.

Let's visualize this with a bookshelf analogy. Imagine a single shelf holding a row of books—this is our one-dimensional list in Python.

```
first_shelf = ["Absolute Beginner's Guide to Python Programming",
               "Pride and Prejudice",
               "Frankenstein",
               "Moby Dick",
               "A Tale of Two Cities"]
```

To retrieve "Moby Dick," which is the 4th book on the shelf, we use its index:

```
print(first_shelf[3])   # Output: Moby Dick
```

Now, a bookshelf typically has more than one shelf. Let's add two more shelves, each with a different number of books, illustrating Python's flexibility:

```
second_shelf = [
    "The Adventures of Huckleberry Finn",
    "Little Women",
    "Sense and Sensibility"
]
third_shelf = [
    "Les Misérables",
    "The Jungle",
    "Persuasion",
    "The Secret Garden",
    "The Wind in the Willows",
    "The Metamorphosis",
    "Dubliners",
    "Beyond Good and Evil"
]
```

## Chapter 3: Exploring Python with Loops and Collections

We can assemble these shelves into a bookshelf, which is a list of lists—a two-dimensional array:

```
bookshelf = [first_shelf,
             second_shelf,
             third_shelf]
```

To access "The Secret Garden" on the third shelf (4th book), we now need two indices:

```
print(bookshelf[2][3])   # Output: The Secret Garden
```

This is how multi-dimensional arrays work in Python. Each list within the outer list can vary in length, just like each shelf can hold a different number of books.

### Adding Books Dynamically to a Shelf

In real life, we often add new books to our shelves. Similarly, in Python, we can dynamically add items to our lists. Let's add a new book to our second shelf:

```
# New book to add
new_book = "The Great Gatsby"

# Add the new book to the second shelf
bookshelf[1].append(new_book)

# Now the second shelf has 4 books
print(f"Updated second shelf: {bookshelf[1]}")
```

The `append()` method adds an element to the end of the list. If we run the above code, our second shelf will now include "The Great Gatsby" as the fourth book.

### Viewing the Entire Bookshelf

To look at our entire bookshelf, we use a `for` loop to iterate over each shelf and then over each book within that shelf:

```
# Iterate over each shelf in the bookshelf
for shelf_number, shelf in enumerate(bookshelf):
    print(f"Shelf {shelf_number} contains:")
    # Iterate over each book in the shelf
    for book in shelf:
```

```
    print(f" - {book}")
print()  # Print a newline for better readability
```

The `enumerate()` function is handy here because it gives us both the index (the shelf number) and the value (the list of books on that shelf). This code will print out each shelf's contents in a structured way, making it easy to see the entire collection at once.

Running this code would give us an output similar to this:

```
Shelf 0 contains:
 - Absolute Beginner's Guide to Python Programming
 - Pride and Prejudice
 - Frankenstein
 - Moby Dick
 - A Tale of Two Cities

Shelf 1 contains:
 - The Adventures of Huckleberry Finn
 - Little Women
 - Sense and Sensibility
 - The Great Gatsby

Shelf 2 contains:
 - Les Misérables
 - The Jungle
 - Persuasion
 - The Secret Garden
 - The Wind in the Willows
 - The Metamorphosis
 - Dubliners
 - Beyond Good and Evil
```

By dynamically adding items and using loops to view our data, we've mimicked managing a real bookshelf, showcasing the power and flexibility of lists in Python. These actions are foundational in many Python programs, especially those involving data collection and manipulation.

## 3.3 Introduction to Tuples

Tuples are very similar to Lists. But they are immutable. Once you create a tuple, it's set. You can't change its contents. Creating a tuple is like creating a list, but instead of square brackets, you use parentheses `()`.

```
point = (5, 10)
print(point[0], point[1])  # Output: 5 10
```

Why use a tuple over a list? Speed and safety. Tuples load faster than lists, making them ideal for storing data that doesn't need changing, like the days of the week or the months of the year. Plus, their immutability (unchangeable nature) protects the data from being altered accidentally.

## When to Use Lists vs. Tuples

Choosing between lists and tuples often comes down to your data's nature and how you plan to use it. Here's a quick guide:

- Choose **lists** when your data collection might change over time, like a to-do list where tasks can be added or removed.

- Choose **tuples** for data that remain constant, where the safety of immutability is beneficial, like the coordinates of a city on a map.

In the end, whether you reach for a list or a tuple depends on the task at hand. Like choosing between a chef's knife and a paring knife, each has its place in your programming toolkit.

As we delve into the world of lists and tuples, we uncover the simplicity and power of Python's data structures. These structures are not just foundational elements, but they empower you to manage and manipulate data in your programs. Lists offer flexibility, allowing your data collection to grow and change, while tuples provide stability and speed for data meant to stay constant. Mastering the usage of these structures is a significant step towards writing more efficient and effective Python code, boosting your confidence in your programming skills.

As you grow more comfortable with lists and tuples, you'll find them indispensable for organizing your data. They're not just the first step in mastering Python's more complex data structures, but they set the stage for deeper data manipulation and analysis. Remember, the goal is not just to write code but to write clear, efficient code that solves problems. Lists and tuples are invaluable allies on this journey, simplifying your approach to data and helping you craft better Python programs. Mastering these structures is an achievement that will inspire and motivate you to explore more complex data structures.

## 3.4 Dictionaries: Mapping Keys to Values

Dictionaries in Python act as containers storing data as key-value pairs. Each key opens the door to its corresponding value, much like a real key opens a lock. Creating a dictionary is akin to drawing a map, where you define destinations and paths. For example, `my_pet = {"name": "Fido", "species": "dog", "age": 5}` constructs a dictionary about a pet, associating each piece of information (value) with a descriptive label (key).

Accessing data in a dictionary is straightforward. Using the key is like telling a GPS system exactly where you want to go, promptly leading you to your destination. If you want to know Fido's age:

```
my_pet = {"name": "Fido",
          "species": "dog",
          "age": 5}
print(my_pet["age"])  # Output: 5
```

This direct access to data elements makes dictionaries incredibly efficient for retrieving information.

## Manipulating Dictionaries

Dictionaries are dynamic; they can evolve. You can add new key-value pairs, offering a way to update your map with new locations. Perhaps Fido has a new favorite toy. Adding this information is simple: `my_pet["fav_toy"] = "rubber bone"`. Now, the dictionary includes this new detail about Fido.

```
my_pet = {"name": "Fido",
          "species": "dog",
          "age": 5}
print(my_pet) # outputs: {'name': 'Fido', 'species': 'dog', 'age': 5}

my_pet["fav_toy"] = "rubber bone"
print(my_pet) # outputs: {'name': 'Fido', 'species': 'dog', 'age': 5, 'fav_toy': 'rubber bone'}
```

But what if a piece of information changes or becomes irrelevant? Python gives you tools to modify or remove entries. Let's say Fido celebrates a birthday. Updating his age is as easy as `my_pet["age"] = 6`.

```
my_pet = {"name": "Fido", "species": "dog", "age": 5}
my_pet["age"] = 6
print(my_pet) # outputs: {'name': 'Fido', 'species': 'dog', 'age': 6}
```

And if, for some reason, the species becomes unnecessary, `del my_pet["species"]` removes it from the dictionary, keeping your data clean and relevant.

```
my_pet = {"name": "Fido", "species": "dog", "age": 5}
del my_pet["species"]
print(my_pet)  # outputs: {'name': 'Fido', 'age': 5}
```

## Practical Use Cases

The real power of dictionaries becomes apparent when applied to practical scenarios. Their structure makes them ideal for representing complex data in a clear and accessible way. Consider a user profile on a social media platform. A dictionary can store varied information about a user, from usernames to interests, in an organized and easily retrievable format. This is invaluable for applications where user-specific data needs to be efficiently managed and accessed.

Dictionaries also excel in settings where relationships between data points are key. In inventory systems, product IDs can serve as keys, leading to values that provide detailed descriptions, prices, and stock levels. This setup ensures that information is not just stored but can be acted upon—whether it's updating stock levels or calculating prices.

## 3.5 Comparing Dictionaries to Lists and Tuples

When deciding between dictionaries, lists, and tuples, consider the nature of your data and how you intend to use it. Lists and tuples are excellent for ordered collections where their position can access items. However, dictionaries offer a clear advantage when dealing with data that is more naturally accessed through unique identifiers (like names, IDs, or titles).

The key-value pairing in dictionaries mirrors how we often store and retrieve information in our minds, making it intuitive for representing real-world data. Unlike lists and tuples, where finding an item requires iterating from the beginning each time, dictionaries allow for immediate access using keys, making data retrieval significantly faster for large collections.

Moreover, the flexibility to update, add, and remove items in dictionaries aligns with dynamic data scenarios. Lists allow similar modifications, but dictionaries provide a structure that directly associates each piece of data with a meaningful label, enhancing clarity and reducing the potential for error.

In contrast, tuples, with their immutable nature, are better suited for fixed collections of items. Their inability to change makes them reliable and efficient, especially for data that serves as a constant throughout your program.

Each of these structures—lists, tuples, and dictionaries—has unique strengths. Lists and tuples offer simplicity and order, ideal for collections of similar items or fixed data sets. Dictionaries, with their direct access and flexibility, excel in handling complex, changeable data where relationships between elements are pivotal. The choice among them depends on your specific needs, balancing factors like the nature of your data, the operations you need to perform, and the importance of order versus accessibility.

## 3.6 Sets: Unleashing the Potential of Unique Collections

In the universe of Python collections, sets stand out for their simplicity and efficiency. Imagine having a bag where each item must be different; no two objects can be the same. This is the essence of sets in Python. They are akin to mathematical sets you might remember from school, designed to hold only unique elements. This unique feature makes sets an invaluable tool in various scenarios, especially when dealing with large datasets where uniqueness is key.

### Introduction to Sets

Sets are created in Python using curly braces `{}` or the `set()` function, and they automatically ensure that all elements within them are distinct. If you try to add a duplicate item to a set, Python quietly ignores the attempt, maintaining the set's unique collection. This behavior is particularly handy when you need to eliminate duplicates from data or when the order of elements is immaterial to your task.

Here's a quick look at how you might create a set:

```python
unique_flavors = {"chocolate", "vanilla", "strawberry", "chocolate"}
print(unique_flavors)  # Outputs: {'chocolate', 'strawberry', 'vanilla'}
```

Notice how "chocolate" is listed twice? When this set is printed, "chocolate" will only appear once because sets allow only unique items.

### Set Operations

Sets support various operations that mirror those you might find in mathematics, providing an intuitive way to compare data collections. These operations include:

- **Union**: Combines two sets into a new set containing all elements from both sets. If both sets have the same item, it will appear only once in the union.

  ```python
  set1 = {"apple", "banana", "cherry"}
  set2 = {"cherry", "date", "fig"}
  union_set = set1.union(set2)
  # or
  union_set = set1 | set2
  print(union_set)  # Outputs: {'banana', 'cherry', 'apple', 'date', 'fig'}
  ```

- **Intersection**: Determines which items are shared between two sets, creating a new set of these common elements.

  ```python
  intersection_set = set1.intersection(set2)
  # or
  intersection_set = set1 & set2
  print(intersection_set)  # Outputs: {'cherry'}
  ```

- **Difference**: This indicates items present in one set but not the other, which is useful for identifying what's unique to a set.

    ```
    difference_set = set1.difference(set2)
    # or
    difference_set = set1 - set2
    print(difference_set)  # Outputs: {'banana', 'apple'}
    ```

- **Symmetric Difference**: Finds items in either of the two sets but not in both, essentially the opposite of intersection.

    ```
    sym_diff_set = set1.symmetric_difference(set2)
    # or
    sym_diff_set = set1 ^ set2
    print(sym_diff_set)  # Outputs: {'banana', 'date', 'apple', 'fig'}
    ```

These operations can be performed with methods or operators, giving you the flexibility to choose the syntax you find more readable.

## Use Cases for Sets

The power of sets is fully realized in scenarios requiring uniqueness or membership checks:

- **Removing Duplicates**: Easily the most straightforward application, converting a list to a set removes any duplicate entries, simplifying your data.

    ```
    response_list = ["yes", "no", "yes", "maybe", "no"]
    unique_responses = set(response_list)
    print(unique_responses)  # Outputs: {'yes', 'no', 'maybe'}
    ```

- **Membership Testing**: Checking if an item is in a set is faster than checking if it's in a list or tuple, especially for large collections. This speed advantage makes sets ideal for quickly determining whether an element exists in your dataset.

    ```
    allowed_users = {"alice", "bob", "charlie"}
    user = "david"
    if user in allowed_users:
        print("Access granted")
    else:
        print("Access denied")  # Outputs: Access denied
    ```

For example, consider a scenario where you're analyzing survey data to find unique responses. Converting the responses list to a set instantly removes any duplicates, leaving you with only unique answers.

## 3.7 Performance Considerations

One of the most compelling reasons to use sets is their performance. Operations like membership testing are significantly faster in sets compared to lists or tuples. This is due to the underlying implementation of sets in Python, which allows for rapid checks on whether an element is contained in the set. This efficiency makes sets an excellent choice for handling large datasets where performance is a concern.

Moreover, the mathematical operations on sets are not just conceptually elegant but also optimized for speed in Python. This means that operations like union, intersection, and difference can be performed quickly, even on large sets. This efficiency opens up new possibilities for data analysis, allowing you to manipulate and compare datasets with ease.

In practice, the performance benefits of sets can have a noticeable impact on your programs. For data-heavy applications, the speed at which sets handle common tasks can lead to more responsive and efficient software. Whether you're filtering duplicate entries from thousands of records or quickly identifying common elements between datasets, sets offer a blend of simplicity and speed that's hard to beat.

In essence, sets in Python provide a unique blend of mathematical rigor and programming convenience. They simplify the task of managing unique collections of items, offering both conceptual clarity and computational efficiency. Whether you're deduplicating data, performing complex analyses, or simply looking for a fast way to check membership, sets are an invaluable tool in your Python toolkit. Their simple syntax, combined with the power of set operations and performance advantages, makes them an essential part of efficient Python programming.

## 3.8 Summarizing Collections

In Python, different types of collections are used to store data in various ways. Each type — lists, tuples, dictionaries, and sets — has its own unique characteristics and is suited to different use cases. Understanding when and why to use each can significantly improve the efficiency and readability of your code. Below is a table summarizing these data structures, highlighting their order, mutability, uniqueness, and typical scenarios where they might be the best choice. This guide will help you choose the right type of collection for your specific programming needs.

## Chapter 3: Exploring Python with Loops and Collections

| Type | Ordered | Mutable | Unique | Use Cases |
|---|---|---|---|---|
| [ ] List | ✓ | ✓ | ✗ | - When you need a collection that can change over time<br>- When the order of elements matters<br>- For storing a sequence of items |
| ( ) Tuple | ✓ | ✗ | ✗ | - When you need a collection that won't change<br>- For storing a sequence of items that should not be modified |
| { : } Dictionary | ✓ | ✓ | ✗ | - When you need to associate values with keys for efficient lookup<br>- For storing data in key/value pairs<br>- Keys are unique, but values are not |
| { } Set | ✗ | ✓ | ✓ | - When you need to ensure no duplicates<br>- For membership testing<br>- For operations like intersection, union and difference |

## 3.9 Loops: The Power of Repetition

In Python, loops bring the magic of automation to life, allowing you to perform repetitive tasks with ease. This is akin to playing your favorite playlist on repeat. Just as the playlist automatically goes back to the first song after the last one finishes, a loop in Python repeats a block of code automatically until a specified condition is met or for a set number of times. This saves you the effort of starting each song manually, just as loops save time and effort in coding by automating repetitive tasks.

### For Loops

The `for` loop in Python is your go-to when you need to iterate over a collection of items, such as a list or a range of numbers. Imagine you have a list of your favorite books and you want to print each title. Rather than writing a print statement for each one, a `for` loop lets you do this in just a few lines:

```
favorite_books = ["Absolute Beginner's Guide to Python Programming",
            "1984", "The Great Gatsby", "The Hobbit"]
for book in favorite_books:
    print(book)
```

Here, the loop runs through each item in `favorite_books`, assigns it to `book`, and prints it. The simplicity and readability of `for` loops make them a favorite among Pythonistas for handling repetitive tasks.

### Using `range()`

The `range()` function generates a sequence of numbers and is particularly useful when you need to execute a loop a specific number of times. It is commonly used in `for` loops to iterate over a sequence of numbers, allowing you to perform an action multiple times. This function is beneficial when you know in advance how many times you need to iterate but do not necessarily have a list of items to iterate over.

```
for i in range(start, stop, step):
    # Perform action
```

- `start`: The starting point of the sequence. This parameter is optional, and if omitted, the sequence starts at 0.
- `stop`: The endpoint of the sequence. The sequence does not include this number.
- `step`: The difference between each number in the sequence. This parameter is optional, and if omitted, the step is 1.

```
for i in range(0, 5):
    print(i)
```

This loop prints numbers from 0 to 4. The `range(0, 5)` generates a sequence of numbers starting from 0 and ending before 5.

## Using `enumerate()`

The `enumerate()` function adds a counter to an iterable and returns it as an enumerate object. This can be directly used in `for` loops to get both the index and the value of each item in the sequence. It is especially useful when you need to have access to the index of each item when looping through a list or any other iterable.

```
for index, value in enumerate(iterable, start=0):
    # Perform action
```

- `iterable`: Any object that supports iteration.
- `start`: The starting index for the counter. This parameter is optional, and if omitted, the counting starts at 0.

```
favorite_books = ["Absolute Beginner's Guide to Python Programming",
                  "1984", "The Great Gatsby", "The Hobbit"]
for index, book in enumerate(favorite_books):
    print(f"{index + 1}: {book}")
```

This loop prints each book in the `favorite_books` list along with its position in the list. The `enumerate(favorite_books)` function provides a convenient way to access both the index (`index`) and the value (`book`) during each iteration.

Both `range()` and `enumerate()` enhance the functionality of `for` loops in Python, offering more control over iteration when dealing with sequences of items. Whether you're iterating a specific number of times with `range()` or accessing index-value pairs with `enumerate()`, these tools make your loops more powerful and expressive.

CHAPTER 3: EXPLORING PYTHON WITH LOOPS AND COLLECTIONS

## 3.10 While Loops

While `for` loops are great for iterating over items, `while` loops shine when you need to execute a block of code as long as a certain condition remains true. A `while` loop keeps running until its condition is no longer met. Consider a scenario where you're saving money for a concert ticket. You might not know how many weeks it'll take to save enough, so a `while` loop is perfect:

```
savings = 0
ticket_price = 100
while savings < ticket_price:
    savings += 25   # Assume you save $25 per week
    print(f"Savings so far: ${savings}")
```

This loop continues to run – and you continue to save – until your savings match or exceed the ticket price. `While` loops are incredibly useful but require careful handling to avoid creating an infinite loop.

## 3.11 Loop Control Statements

Sometimes, you might need more control over your loop's execution. This is where loop control statements like `break`, `continue`, and `else` come into play.

- `break` lets you exit a loop when a particular condition is met. It's like telling your coffee maker to stop brewing if it runs out of water.

- `continue` skips the rest of the loop's body for the current iteration and moves on to the next one. It's akin to skipping a particular song in a playlist but continuing with the rest.

- `else` in loops is a bit different from its use in conditional statements. It executes a block of code after the loop completes but only if the loop wasn't terminated by a `break`.

Here's an example to illustrate `break` and `continue`:

```
for number in range(1, 11):
    if number == 5:
        continue  # Skip printing the number 5
    if number > 7:
        break  # Stop the loop if the number is greater than 7
    print(number)
```

This loop prints numbers 1 to 4, skips 5, and then prints 6 and 7 before the `break` stops the loop.

## 3.12 Nesting Loops

Nesting loops means placing one loop inside another. This technique can be incredibly powerful for certain tasks, like iterating over multi-dimensional data structures. Picture a list of lists, where each inner list represents a different category of expenses for a budget. To go through each expense in each category, you'd use a nested loop:

```
expenses = [
    [250, 150, 60],   # Category 1 expenses
    [80, 20],         # Category 2 expenses
    [100, 200, 150]   # Category 3 expenses
]

for category in expenses:
    print("New category:")
    for expense in category:
        print(expense)
```

Here, the outer loop iterates over each category, and the inner loop iterates over each expense within that category. While nesting loops are powerful, it's also where complexity can ramp up quickly. Deeply nested loops can make your code harder to follow and debug. It's often worth exploring if the task at hand can be simplified or if there's a more Pythonic way to achieve the same result.

Loops in Python, with their ability to automate and simplify repetitive tasks, are indispensable. Whether iterating over items with a `for` loop, running a block of code until a condition changes with a `while` loop, or controlling the flow of execution with loop control statements, these structures enhance the functionality and efficiency of your code. Moreover, understanding when and how to nest loops opens up even more possibilities, allowing you to work effectively with complex data structures. With these tools, you're well-equipped to tackle a wide range of programming tasks, making your code not just functional but elegant.

## 3.13 Chapter Summary

In Chapter 3, we explored Python's collections and loops, equipping you with the foundational tools for data organization, access, and manipulation.

By exploring the intricacies of lists, tuples, dictionaries, and sets, we uncovered the vital roles these structures play in Python's approach to data management. Through practical examples, we demonstrated how lists and tuples serve as versatile containers, dictionaries offer efficient key-value storage and sets ensure uniqueness within your data collections.

CHAPTER 3: EXPLORING PYTHON WITH LOOPS AND COLLECTIONS

Moreover, the exploration of `for` and `while` loops introduced the mechanisms for iterating over these collections and executing code repetitively based on conditions, thus automating tasks and enhancing program efficiency.

---

## 3.14 Suggested Exercises

### Exercise 1: List Manipulation

**Description**: This exercise will help you practice basic list operations such as adding, removing, and modifying elements. You will create a list of your favorite movies, add new movies, remove one, and print the updated list.

**Task**: Create a list of your favorite movies. Add two more movies, remove one, and print the updated list.

### Exercise 2: 2D Array Access

**Description**: Learn to work with multi-dimensional arrays (lists of lists) by creating a 3x3 matrix and accessing its elements using nested loops. This exercise will enhance your understanding of how to iterate over complex data structures.

**Task**: Create a 3x3 matrix and print each element using nested loops.

### Exercise 3: Dictionary Operations

**Description**: This exercise focuses on dictionary operations such as adding, updating, and accessing values. You will create a dictionary to store information about a book, update its values, and print all keys and values.

**Task**: Create a dictionary with information about a book (title, author, year). Add a key for genre, update the year, and print all the keys and values.

### Exercise 4: Set Operations

**Description**: Practice working with sets by creating a set of unique words from a given sentence. This exercise will help you understand how sets handle uniqueness and membership operations.

**Task**: Create a set of unique words from a given sentence.

## Exercise 5: For Loop Practice

**Description**: Gain experience with for loops by writing a loop that generates the first 10 numbers in the Fibonacci sequence. This exercise will enhance your understanding of iterative processes and sequence generation.

**Task**: Write a for loop to print the first 10 numbers in the Fibonacci sequence.

## Exercise 6: While Loop Practice

**Description**: This exercise will help you practice while loops by writing a loop to reverse a string. You will gain a better understanding of condition-based iteration and string manipulation.

**Task**: Write a while loop to reverse a string.

## Exercise 7: Combined Data Types

**Description**: Learn to work with combined data types by creating a list of dictionaries. Each dictionary will represent a student with keys for name and grade. You will print each student's name and grade using a loop.

**Task**: Create a list of dictionaries, where each dictionary represents a student with keys for name and grade. Print each student's name and grade using a loop.

---

# 3.15 Project: Build a Python Quiz Game

This next project is a Quiz Game, further solidifying your understanding of collections and loops by applying these concepts in a fun, interactive way. This project tests your knowledge and encourages creative problem-solving and coding practice.

**Objective:** Create an interactive quiz game that tests the player's knowledge across various topics. The game should present a series of questions, each with multiple-choice answers, and track the player's score throughout the session."

## Setup Instructions

1. **Define Questions and Answers:**
    - Create a list of dictionaries, where each dictionary represents a quiz question, its multiple-choice options, and the correct answer.

Since the focus of the project isn't to test your creativity, I will provide you with some questions below. Use them, or don't use them. Either works.

2. **Gameplay Flow:**
   o Display a welcome message to the user.
   o Loop through the questions.

   *Optionally*: You could randomly shuffle the questions to ensure a unique gameplay experience each time. To do so, you would need to import Python's `random` package and then shuffle the questions. We haven't talked about importing Python packages, so here is the code to do it:

   ```
   # Shuffle the questions
   import random
   random.shuffle(questions)
   ```

   o Iterate through the questions, presenting each one to the user along with the answer choices.
   o Prompt the user for their answer to each question.

3. **Scoring:**
   o Keep track of the user's score by incrementing it for each correct answer.
   o Provide immediate feedback to the user after each question, indicating whether their answer was correct or incorrect. If incorrect, display the correct answer.

4. **Ending the Game:**
   o Allow the user to exit the game early by typing a specific command (e.g., 'exit').
   o Once all questions have been answered, or the user decides to exit, display the user's final score.

## Success Criteria

- The game must successfully run without errors.
- The user should be able to select their answer to each question and receive immediate feedback.
- The game should accurately track and display the user's score.
- The game should offer an option for the user to exit at any point.

## Setting Up for Success

- **Review Collections:** Understand how lists and dictionaries can store quiz questions and options.
- **Practice Loops:** Familiarize yourself with `for` and `while` loops for iterating through the questions and validating user inputs.

- **Input and Output:** Get comfortable with using `input()` to capture user responses and `print()` to display messages and questions.

## Sample Quiz Questions

Question 1: Who was buried in Andrew Jackson's grave?

- Options:
    1. Donald Trump
    2. Andrew Jackson
    3. John Tyler
    4. Joe Biden
- Correct Answer: Andrew Jackson

Question 2: What color was George Washington's great white horse?

- Options:
    1. Black
    2. Brown
    3. White
    4. Green
- Correct Answer: White

Question 3: What data type is used to store items as a sequence that can maintain order?

- Options:
    1. List
    2. Tuple
    3. Set
    4. Dictionary
- Correct Answer: List

Question 4: To loop over each character in a word, which Python structure should you use?

- Options:
    1. For loop
    2. While loop
    3. If statement
    4. Print Statement
- Correct Answer: For loop

Question 5: Which Python collection allows us to store unique items identified by a key?

- Options:
  1. List
  2. Tuple
  3. Set
  4. Dictionary
- Correct Answer: Dictionary

Question 6: Which Python collection type prevents duplicates?

- Options:
  1. List
  2. Tuple
  3. Set
  4. Dictionary
- Correct Answer: Set

This project is designed to reinforce your understanding of Python's fundamental concepts while also providing a fun and interactive way to engage with the material. Remember, the key to success is not just completing the project but learning and experimenting with Python along the way.

## Example of Possible Output

```
Welcome to the Basic Quiz Game!

1/6: What data type is used to store items as a sequence that can maintain order?
1. List
2. Tuple
3. Set
4. Dictionary
Your answer (1-4): 1
Correct! You earned a point.

2/6: What color was George Washington's great white horse?
1. Black
2. Brown
3. White
4. Green
Your answer (1-4): 3
Correct! You earned a point.

3/6: Who was buried in Andrew Jackson grave?
1. Donald Trump
2. Andrew Jackson
3. John Tyler
4. Joe Biden
Your answer (1-4): 2
Correct! You earned a point.
```

```
4/6: Which Python collection type prevents duplicates?
1. List
2. Tuple
3. Set
4. Dictionary
Your answer (1-4): 3
Correct! You earned a point.

5/6: To loop over each character in a word, which Python structure should you use?
1. For loop
2. While loop
3. If statement
4. Print Statement
Your answer (1-4): 1
Correct! You earned a point.

6/6: Which Python collection allows us to store unique items identified by a key?
1. List
2. Tuple
3. Set
4. Dictionary
Your answer (1-4): 1
```

# Chapter 4: The Power of Functions, Modules, Packages and Lambdas

In this chapter, we delve into the essential building blocks that elevate your Python programming from simple scripts to robust and scalable applications. By mastering functions, you encapsulate tasks into reusable units, enhancing code modularity and efficiency. Modules extend this organization, allowing you to group related functions, variables, and classes, facilitating code reuse and clarity. Lambda functions introduce a layer of succinctness, enabling you to write anonymous functions for quick, in-line operations. Together, these elements form the cornerstone of Python programming, empowering you to write cleaner, more efficient, and maintainable code.

## 4.1 Functions

In Python, functions are the essential building blocks for structuring and reusing code. They allow you to encapsulate a task into a single, coherent unit of work that can be used repeatedly throughout your program. Understanding functions is key to writing clean, efficient, and modular code.

CHAPTER 4: THE POWER OF FUNCTIONS, MODULES, PACKAGES AND LAMBDAS

## Creating Functions

A function is defined using the `def` keyword, followed by the function name and parentheses `()` which may include parameters. The code block within the function starts with a colon `:` and is indented.

```
def greet(name):
    print(f"Hello, {name}!")
```

## Calling Functions

To execute a function, you use the function name followed by parentheses. If the function expects arguments, you provide them inside the parentheses.

```
greet("Alice")
```

## Passing and Returning Values

When you define a function, you might specify parameters that allow you to pass information to it. These parameters act as placeholders for the actual values, or arguments, you provide when you call the function. This mechanism enables you to execute a function with different data, making your functions more flexible and reusable.

Moreover, functions aren't limited to performing actions; they can also return results using the `return` keyword. This feature is particularly useful when you need the output of a function for further computation or decision-making in your program. For instance:

```
def add_numbers(num1, num2):
    return num1 + num2
```

Here, `add_numbers` accepts two arguments, adds them, and returns the result, which can then be used elsewhere in your program.

## Default Parameters

A powerful feature of Python functions is the ability to define functions with default parameters. Default parameters allow you to assign a default value to a parameter that will be used if no argument is passed for it when the function is called. This makes your functions even more flexible, allowing them to be called with fewer arguments than they are defined to accept.

Default parameters are defined by assigning values in the function declaration. For example:

```
def greet(name, message="Hello"):
    print(f"{message}, {name}!")
```

In this `greet` function, `name` is a required parameter, while `message` is optional with a default value of `"Hello"`. This allows the function to be called in two ways:

```
greet("Jasmin")                # Uses the default message: "Hello, Jasmin!"
greet("Bob", "Good morning")   # Uses a custom message: "Good morning, Bob!"
```

This feature is particularly useful for functions that have options that are frequently not specified because they have common defaults. It also helps in reducing the amount of code needed for function calls, making your code cleaner and more readable.

When using default parameters, any parameters with default values must be defined after those without defaults in the function's signature. This is to ensure that Python knows which parameter you're referring to when the function is called.

## 4.2 Scope and Lifetime of Variables

The concept of scope is crucial when working with functions. It determines where in your program a variable can be accessed. Variables defined inside a function have a local scope, meaning they can only be accessed within that function. Conversely, variables defined outside of any function have a global scope, making them accessible throughout the program.

The lifetime of a variable refers to how long it exists in memory. For local variables, this duration is limited to the time the function is executing. Once the function completes, these variables are discarded, making them temporary placeholders that help the function perform its task without affecting the rest of your program.

Understanding scope and lifetime helps prevent conflicts and errors in your code, ensuring that each function interacts with the rest of your program in a predictable manner.

## 4.3 Global Variables

In Python, variables have a scope, which determines where they can be accessed or modified in your code. Up to this point, we've focused on local variables—variables that are defined inside a function and can only be used within that function. Now, let's introduce another type: global variables.

### What is a Global Variable?

A global variable is a variable that is defined outside of any function, making it accessible throughout the entire program. This means you can read or modify the variable from any function or part of your code. Global variables are often used to store information that needs to be shared or accessed by multiple parts of a program.

CHAPTER 4: THE POWER OF FUNCTIONS, MODULES, PACKAGES AND LAMBDAS

## Defining and Using Global Variables

Let's look at an example to see how a global variable works:

```python
# Define a global variable
counter = 0

def increment_counter():
    global counter  # Declare the global variable inside the function
    counter += 1    # Modify the global variable
    print(f"Counter after increment: {counter}")

increment_counter()  # Output: Counter after increment: 1
increment_counter()  # Output: Counter after increment: 2
```

## Key Points:

- **Declaration**: A global variable is declared outside of any function.
- **Access and Modification**: To modify a global variable within a function, you must use the global keyword. This tells Python that you are referring to the variable defined outside the function, not creating a new local variable.

## Why Use Global Variables?

Global variables can be useful in situations where multiple functions need to access or modify the same data. For example, in a game, a global variable could be used to keep track of the player's score across different levels.

However, global variables should be used sparingly because they can make your code harder to read and debug. Here are some scenarios where global variables might be appropriate:

- **Program State Management**: Storing the state of a program, such as user settings or configurations, that should persist and be available to all functions.
- **Counters or Accumulators**: Keeping track of counts or totals that multiple functions need to update.

## Caution: Pitfalls of Using Global Variables

While global variables can be useful, overusing them can lead to some problems:

- **Unintended Changes**: If many functions can change a global variable, it can be difficult to trace where or why a value was modified, leading to bugs.
- **Reduced Code Clarity**: Code that relies heavily on global variables may be harder to read and understand, especially in larger projects.
- **Limited Reusability**: Functions that depend on global variables are less flexible and harder to reuse in different contexts.

## Best Practices for Global Variables

To avoid these pitfalls, here are some best practices for using global variables:

- **Minimize Usage**: Use global variables only when necessary. Prefer passing variables as parameters to functions or returning values from functions.

- **Descriptive Naming**: Give global variables meaningful names that clearly indicate their purpose. This helps make the code easier to read and maintain.

- **Encapsulation**: Consider encapsulating related global variables within a class or a specific module. This can help group them logically and reduce the risk of unintended side effects.

## Practical Example: Using Global Variables in a Simple Game

Let's see a practical example where global variables can be useful. Imagine you are building a simple game where you need to keep track of the player's score.

```python
score = 0  # Global variable to keep track of the score

def add_points(points):
    global score
    score += points
    print(f"Score updated! New score: {score}")

def reset_score():
    global score
    score = 0
    print("Score reset!")

add_points(10)   # Adds 10 points
add_points(5)    # Adds 5 more points
reset_score()    # Resets the score
```

In this example, the global variable score is used by multiple functions (add_points and reset_score) to manage the game's scoring system.

## When to Avoid Global Variables

Global variables should be avoided in the following scenarios:

- **Complex Programs**: For large, complex applications, global variables can lead to tightly coupled code, making it difficult to maintain and scale.

- **Multi-threaded Programs**: In concurrent or multi-threaded applications, global variables can create race conditions, where multiple threads try to modify the same variable simultaneously, leading to unpredictable behavior.

Global variables are useful for storing information that needs to be accessed across multiple functions or modules. However, they should be used with caution to avoid unintended side effects and to maintain the readability and maintainability of your code. By following best practices, you can leverage global variables effectively when needed.

## 4.4 Modules

Modules in Python are essential for organizing functions, variables, and classes into separate files. This organization improves code readability and manageability, facilitates code reuse, and ensures clear namespace separation.

### Creating a Module

A Python file with a .py extension is considered a module. Within this file, you can define functions, variables, and classes, which can then be imported and used in other Python scripts. For example, let's create a simple module:

```python
# mymodule.py
def say_hello(name):
    print(f"Hello, {name}!")
```

### Using Modules

To use the module you've created, employ the `import` statement to bring any definitions from the module into your current script.

```python
import mymodule
mymodule.say_hello("Bob")
```

### The `if __name__ == "__main__":` Idiom

One important aspect of Python modules is determining whether the module is being run as the main program or being imported into another script. This is where the `if __name__ == "__main__":` idiom comes into play:

```python
# mymodule.py
def say_hello(name):
    print(f"Hello, {name}!")

if __name__ == "__main__":
    # Code block that runs only when the module is executed directly
    say_hello("Sofia")
```

When `mymodule.py` is run directly, the code under `if __name__ == "__main__":` executes.

This allows a module to serve dual purposes: as a reusable module imported by other scripts, and as a standalone program for testing or direct execution.

## Significance of Double Underscores (__) in Python

The double underscores (also known as "dunders") in variable names like `__name__` are used for special or "magic" variables and methods that Python uses internally. These are not meant for regular use in your code but are designed to help Python's interpreter differentiate between user-defined items and its internal system.

- **`__name__`**: This is a special built-in variable in every Python module. When a module is run directly, Python sets `__name__` to "`__main__`". When the same module is imported into another script, `__name__` is set to the module's name. This distinction allows for conditional execution based on how the module is being used.
- **Why Use Double Underscores?** Using double underscores helps prevent naming conflicts between user-defined variables and Python's built-in functionalities. It separates internal Python mechanisms from the code you write, enhancing clarity and reducing the risk of accidental overriding.

## Best Practices for Organizing Modules

- **Naming Conventions:** Use clear, descriptive names for modules. Python module names should be lowercase, with underscores to separate words if necessary to improve readability.
- **Logical Structure:** Organize related functions, classes, and variables within the same module. This logical grouping not only makes your code more navigable but also simplifies maintenance and extension.
- **Reuse and Namespace Separation:** Use modules to reuse code effectively across different parts of your project. This approach helps avoid name clashes and keeps your codebase well-organized.

# 4.5 Packages

Python packages offer a more advanced level of organization beyond single-file modules, enabling the structuring of Python's module namespace using "dotted module names". A package is essentially a directory that contains a special file named `__init__.py`, which may also include one or more modules or even sub-packages.

## Creating a Package

Organizing a set of related modules into a package can significantly enhance the maintainability and scalability of your projects. For instance, if you are developing features related to handling user information, such as profiles and permissions, these can be organized into a package for better structure.

1. Create a Directory: Name the directory after your package, such as `user`. This name will be used to import the package or its modules into other parts of your application.

2. Add `__init__.py`: Inside the `user` directory, add an `__init__.py` file. This file can be empty, but it signals to Python that this directory should be treated as a package.

3. Include Modules: Move your related modules, like `user_profile.py` and `user_permissions.py`, into the directory.

## Using Packages

To utilize the modules within your package, you can import them using the package name followed by the module name. This approach allows you to access functions, classes, and variables defined within those modules in a structured manner.

```
from user import user_profile
user_profile.create_profile("Alice")
```

## Relative Imports

Within a package, modules can use relative imports to access sibling modules. This can make it easier to refactor and move around modules without breaking imports. For example, if `user_profile.py` needs to import a function from `user_permissions.py`, you can use:

```
from .user_permissions import some_permission_function
```

The leading dot (.) indicates a relative import that starts in the same directory as the module making the import.

## Best Practices for Organizing Modules and Packages

- Clarity and Simplicity in Function Design: Ensure functions within your modules and packages have a clear purpose and perform a single task to improve readability and maintainability.

- Descriptive Naming: Choose names that reflect the purpose and contents of your modules and packages, facilitating easier navigation and understanding of your codebase.

- Logical Structure: Organize related functions into modules and group related modules into packages. This not only makes your code more navigable but also simplifies its extension and maintenance.

- Utilize `__init__.py` for Package Initialization: Beyond simply signaling that a directory is a package, `__init__.py` can also be used to perform package-level initialization tasks, such as setting up package-wide data or importing necessary modules for the package's internal use.

Packages in Python are a powerful mechanism for structuring and organizing your code, allowing for scalable and maintainable project development. By effectively using modules for organization and packages for module grouping, along with adhering to best practices in design and structure, you create a robust foundation for your projects that can accommodate growth and complexity.

## 4.6 Lambda Functions

Lambda functions, or anonymous functions, are a concise way to create small functions in Python. Defined with the `lambda` keyword, they can accept any number of arguments but are limited to a single expression. The simplicity and concise syntax of lambda functions make them ideal for straightforward tasks where a full function definition would be unnecessarily verbose.

### Why Use Lambda Functions?

Lambda functions are perfect for short-lived operations, especially within higher-order functions like `sorted()`, `filter()`, and `map()` that take functions as arguments. They enable you to write cleaner and more readable code for operations that are easily expressed in a single line.

### Structure of Lambda Functions

The syntax for a lambda function is as follows:

```
lambda arguments: expression
```

- `lambda`: This keyword initiates the anonymous function.
- `arguments`: Similar to arguments in standard functions, these are the inputs to your lambda function. They can be a single argument, multiple arguments separated by commas, or none at all.
- `expression`: A single expression that is evaluated and returned by the function. This can perform operations on the arguments and include arithmetic, logical operations, and more.

### Simple Example of Lambda: Multiplying Numbers

Consider a lambda function that multiplies two numbers:

CHAPTER 4: THE POWER OF FUNCTIONS, MODULES, PACKAGES AND LAMBDAS

```
multiply = lambda x, y: x * y
print(multiply(2, 3))   # Output: 6
```

This demonstrates how a lambda function can succinctly perform an operation on two arguments.

## Ideal Usages of Lambda

Lambda functions are best suited for operations that can be expressed in a single line. For example, in a loan calculator program, calculating monthly payments can be succinctly done with a lambda:

```
payment = lambda P, r, n: P * (r * (1 + r) ** n) / ((1 + r) ** n - 1)
monthly_payment = payment(100000, 0.05/12, 10*12)
print(f"Monthly Payment: ${monthly_payment:.2f}")
```

## 4.7 Enhancing Lambda Functions with `filter`, `map`, and `sorted`

Lambda functions shine when used in conjunction with higher-order functions like `filter`, `map`, and `sorted`. These functions take another function as an argument, making lambda functions their perfect companion for concise and readable code.

### Using `filter` with Lambda Functions

The `filter()` function is used to create an iterator from elements of an iterable for which a function returns true. In combination with a lambda function, `filter()` can succinctly filter items in a collection. For example:

```
numbers = [1, 2, 3, 4, 5, 6]
even_numbers = list(filter(lambda x: x % 2 == 0, numbers))
print(even_numbers)   # Output: [2, 4, 6]
```

### Using `map` with Lambda Functions

The `map()` function applies a given function to all items in an input list. A lambda function used with `map()` allows simple transformations to be applied to each element in the collection. For example:

```
numbers = [1, 2, 3, 4, 5]
squared_numbers = list(map(lambda x: x**2, numbers))
print(squared_numbers)   # Output: [1, 4, 9, 16, 25]
```

## Sorting with Lambda Functions

The `sorted()` function sorts the items of a given iterable in a specific order (default is ascending) and returns a new sorted list. Lambda functions can be used as the `key` argument in `sorted()` to define custom sorting logic. For example:

```
fruits = [('apple', 2), ('orange', 5), ('banana', 1)]
sorted_fruits = sorted(fruits, key=lambda x: x[1])
print(sorted_fruits) # Output: [('banana', 1), ('apple', 2), ('orange', 5)]
```

### NERD NOTES  *The Lambda Hammer Effect*

*When you're new to coding—and you finally understand lambdas—it feels like discovering a magical new tool. Suddenly, every problem looks like it can be solved with this shiny little one-liner.*

*This phenomenon is so common that there's even a saying: "When all you have is a hammer, everything looks like a nail." In Python, that hammer is sometimes called lambda.*

*But here's the truth: just because you can use a lambda doesn't mean you should. Often, a regular* `def` *function is clearer, easier to test, and more maintainable.*

*Lambdas are like hot sauce—when used right, they add just the right kick. But use too much, and suddenly you're hating life, sweating through the code: heat for the sake of heat, wondering what happened to the flavor.*

## Best Practices with Lambda Functions

- **Use Sparingly:** For more complex or reusable code, a full function definition is preferable for the sake of readability and maintainability.
- **Readability Matters:** If using a lambda function complicates understanding the code, consider defining a regular function.
- **Keep It Simple:** Lambda functions are designed to be simple one-liners. Anything more complex should be articulated through a defined function.

Lambda functions in Python offer a streamlined way to perform simple operations and are particularly effective when used in conjunction with higher-order functions. Understanding when and how to use lambda functions can greatly enhance the readability and efficiency of your Python code. However, it's important to balance their convenience with the overall clarity of your code, opting for traditional function definitions when complexity increases.

## 4.8 Chapter Summary

Throughout this chapter, we've explored the fundamentals and intricacies of functions, modules, and lambda expressions in Python. Starting with functions, we learned how to define, call, and pass information to them and how they can return values, enhancing the modularity and reusability of our code. We then expanded our toolkit by organizing these functions into modules, making our projects more navigable and manageable. Packages were introduced as a means to structure our codebase further, using "dotted module names" for namespace organization.

Lambda functions were highlighted for their ability to perform operations in a concise manner, ideal for short-lived tasks that complement higher-order functions like `sorted()`, `filter()`, and `map()`. We demonstrated their effectiveness in simplifying code for operations such as multiplying numbers, sorting data, and more through practical examples.

## 4.9 Suggested Exercises

### Exercise 1: Basic Function Creation

**Description**: Practice creating functions that perform simple tasks.

**Task**: Write a function that takes a list of numbers and returns the sum of the numbers.

### Exercise 2: Scope and Lifetime

**Description**: Understand variable scope by working with global and local variables.

**Task**: Write a function that modifies a global variable and another function that uses a local variable with the same name.

### Exercise 3: Using Standard Modules

**Description**: Practice importing and using standard library modules.

**Task**: Write a script that uses the `math` module to calculate the area of a circle given its radius.

### Exercise 4: Creating and Importing Custom Modules

**Description**: Learn to create and import custom modules.

**Task**: Create a custom module with a function that checks if a number is prime and use it in a script.

## Exercise 5: Working with Packages

**Description**: Understand the structure and use of packages.

**Task**: Create a package with multiple modules and use them in a script.

## Exercise 6: Lambda Functions

**Description**: Practice creating and using lambda functions.

**Task**: Write a script that uses a lambda function to sort a list of tuples by the second element.

---

# 4.10 Project: Tic-Tac-Toe Game

In this project, you'll build a Tic-Tac-Toe game. A simple yet engaging game that serves as an excellent introduction to the fundamentals of programming. Known globally as "Noughts and Crosses" in the UK and "Xs and Os" in Canada and Ireland, this game's universal appeal lies in its simplicity and the strategic thinking it requires.

In this section, we'll build a basic version of Tic-Tac-Toe where two human players can compete against each other. By coding this game, you'll learn about controlling game flow, managing state, and the basics of user interaction—all crucial skills for any budding programmer.

## Understanding Game Flow

Before we dive into coding, it's important to understand the flow of Tic-Tac-Toe. Here's a simplified flowchart to help visualize the game's process:

```
Start
  ↓
Initialize Board
  ↓
Player 1 Input → Validate Move → Update Board
  ↓
Check for Win or Draw
  ↓
Switch Player
  ↓
Repeat Until Win or Draw
  ↓
End
```

CHAPTER 4: THE POWER OF FUNCTIONS, MODULES, PACKAGES AND LAMBDAS

Each part of this flow represents a step we'll implement. Using Python, we will handle player inputs, validate moves, update the game state, and determine the outcome of the game.

### Core Concepts to Implement

- **Board Initialization**: Setting up a 3x3 grid.
- **Player Turns**: Alternating turns between Player X and Player O.
- **Move Validation**: Ensuring the chosen position is valid.
- **Win Condition Check**: Determining if a player has won.
- **Draw Condition Check**: Detecting a tie if no spaces are left.

Later in this chapter, we will enhance this first version to include AI. Then in Chapter 7 – "Graphical User Interfaces with Tkinter", we will convert it from a console-based application to a GUI.

### Project Requirements

The game should:

- Allow two players to play Tic-Tac-Toe.
- Enable players to input their moves.
- Validate moves to ensure they are legal.
- Announce a winner or declare a draw.

## 4.11 Game Design and Flow

### Board Representation

The game board is represented as a list of strings, where each string can be "X", "O", or empty to signify an available spot. The board starts off entirely empty, like this:

```
board = [" ", " ", " ", " ", " ", " ", " ", " ", " "]
```

or a more concise version of the same thing by using a single list with nine empty string spaces, using list multiplication for a concise setup:

```
board = [" "] * 9
```

Visual representation of the board:

```
 0 | 1 | 2
---+---+---
 3 | 4 | 5
```

```
---+---+---
 6 | 7 | 8
```

## 4.12 Step-by-Step Guide to Building the Game

### Step 1: Implement `game_mechanics.py`

Create functions to initialize the board, check for a winner, and check for a draw.

1. **Initialize the Board**:

    o   Purpose: Create a list containing an empty board.
    o   **Implementation Tip**: Returns an empty board with a statement like this: `return [" "] * 9`

2. **Check for Game Draw function**:

    o   Purpose: Create a method that checks if the game has ended in a draw (i.e., the board is full, and no spaces are left).
    o   Implementation Tip: Iterate over the board to see if any cells are still empty. Return `True` if none are found; otherwise, return `False`.

    A slick Pythonic approach would be: `return " " not in board`

    `board` is a list variable containing the board.

3. **Check for Game Winner function**:

    o   Purpose: Write a method to determine if a player has won the game.
    o   Implementation Tip: Define all possible winning combinations (rows, columns, diagonals). See the "Winning Positions" image. Check if any combination has the same player symbol across all its cells. Return the winning player symbol if a win is detected; otherwise, return `None`.

# Chapter 4: The Power of Functions, Modules, Packages and Lambdas

## Step 2: Implement `game_ui.py`

This step involves creating the user interface for your Tic-Tac-Toe game. We will write functions to display the game board and to handle player input effectively.

1. **Display the Board:**
    - **Purpose:** Display the current state of the game board in a user-friendly format.
    - **Implementation Tip:** Use print statements to display the board as a grid. Each cell can be accessed via its index in the list, and you should include lines to separate the rows.
2. **Get Human Player Move:**
    - **Purpose:** Obtain and validate the current player's move. Ensure the selected move is valid (i.e., the chosen cell is empty and within the board's range).
    - **Implementation Tip:** Prompt the player for their move using input and check if the selected position is valid. The function should handle invalid inputs gracefully and prompt the player again if necessary. Consider using a loop to keep asking for input until a valid move is made.

These functions form the core of your game's user interface, handling both the display of the game state and the interaction with the players. Ensure these functions are robust and user-friendly to provide a smooth gameplay experience.

## Step 3: Implement `main.py`

Tie everything together using a main function that controls the game flow. This diagram represents the game flow implemented in the book's version:

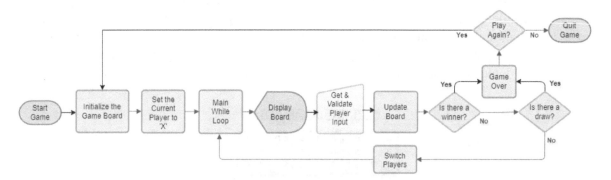

## Take a Game Break!

Now that you've successfully built your very own Tic-Tac-Toe game, it's time to put it to the test! Go ahead and take a well-deserved break—challenge a friend or family member to a few rounds. Playing your game helps solidify what you've learned and allows you to enjoy the fruits of your labor.

Experience firsthand how your code translates into a fun and interactive game. Observe how the game flows, make notes of any unexpected behavior, and think about what could be improved. This hands-on experience is invaluable as you continue your journey in learning programming.

Once you feel comfortable with how everything is working, you'll be ready to tackle the next exciting challenge: introducing an AI opponent. Get ready to elevate your game to the next level!

## 4.13 Introducing an AI Opponent

Now that you've mastered creating a game where two human players can challenge each other, let's elevate your programming skills and Tic-Tac-Toe game by introducing an artificial intelligence (AI) opponent. Integrating AI will make your game playable against the computer and introduce you to fundamental concepts of game AI.

### AI Implementation and Strategy

In this phase, you'll implement a simple rules-based AI that can make decisions based on the game's current state. The AI will attempt to win or block you from winning, and when those options aren't available, it will make strategic moves to position itself advantageously.

- **Primary Objective**: The AI should aim to win by checking potential moves for a win on the next turn.
- **Secondary Objective**: If a win isn't imminent, the AI should check if it needs to block your potential winning move.
- **Strategic Moves**: If neither winning nor blocking is possible, the AI should choose a strategic position, typically the center or corners, as these are generally the best spots for future moves.

### Strategy Breakdown

- **Winning Strategy**: The AI evaluates each empty spot on the board; if placing its symbol there results in a win, it will do so.
- **Blocking Strategy**: If the AI can't win immediately, it checks if you are about to win and places its symbol to block you.
- **Positional Strategy**: Prioritizing corners and the center if neither winning nor blocking moves are available.
- **Random Play**: As a fallback, the AI chooses a random empty spot. This ensures that the gameplay remains unpredictable and fun.

## Implementation Details

We will extend the `game_ai.py` to include new functions that support AI decision-making:

- **Test Move Functionality**: This function will simulate the game board after a move to determine if it results in a win.
- **Rules-Based AI Decision Function**: Implements the AI logic that decides the best move based on the current board state.

```
def get_rules_based_ai_move(computer_player, board):
    # Winning, blocking, and strategic logic as previously described
```

## 4.14 Step-by-Step Guide to Building the AI

- **Step 1: Implement Test Moves Function**: Create a function in `game_ai.py` to simulate placing a symbol in each possible position and checking the outcome.
- **Step 2: Develop AI Decision Logic**: Write the AI's decision-making logic that evaluates the board and determines the optimal move based on the strategies described.
- **Step 3: Integrate AI into Main Game Loop**: Modify `main.py` to incorporate AI moves when it's the computer's turn to play.

```
if current_player == computer_player:
    move = get_rules_based_ai_move(computer_player, board)
else:
    move = get_human_player_move(current_player, board)
```

## Testing and Adjustments

Once implemented, play several rounds against your AI to evaluate its effectiveness. Based on your observations, adjust its decision-making process to make the gameplay challenging yet fair.

## Next Steps

Consider this AI integration as an introduction to the vast field of game AI. You can further enhance this AI with more sophisticated algorithms or even explore machine learning techniques to make your AI learn from each game.

## Take Another Game Break!

After implementing your AI, take another game break to test your enhanced Tic-Tac-Toe. Enjoy competing against your creation, and pay attention to how it makes its decisions. This direct interaction will help you understand its strengths and limitations.

Enjoy the process of seeing your Tic-Tac-Toe game come to life with AI, and get ready to delve deeper into the exciting world of artificial intelligence in gaming!

## 4.15 Explore Advanced AI Techniques

For avid learners and budding game developers eager to delve deeper into the world of artificial intelligence, our GitHub repository offers a special extension to the Tic-Tac-Toe project you've just completed. While this book introduces basic AI concepts suitable for beginners, we've prepared additional materials online for those ready to take their skills to the next level.

### Advanced AI Versions Available Online

On GitHub, you'll find two additional AI versions designed for Tic-Tac-Toe: Random AI and MinMax AI. The Random AI introduces an element of unpredictability, making random moves and providing a fun yet simple alternative to strategic gameplay. In contrast, the MinMax AI embodies a more strategic and calculated approach, making it a formidable opponent. It is a bit more sophisticated than the Rules-Based AI we just built earlier.

### Understanding MinMax AI

The MinMax algorithm is a decision-making tool used in game theory to determine the optimal move for a player, assuming that the opponent is also playing optimally. Here's how it works:

- **MinMax Basics**: The algorithm simulates all possible moves in the game, then evaluates the game state to assign scores to each move. For Tic-Tac-Toe, this might involve calculating whether a move leads to a win, a loss, or a draw.
- **Optimization**: The 'Min' part of the algorithm assumes the worst-case scenario—loss, and it tries to minimize that possibility. Conversely, the 'Max' part looks for the move that maximizes the player's chances of winning.
- **Recursive Evaluation**: MinMax uses a recursive approach, where the function calls itself, alternating between minimizing and maximizing until it reaches a terminal state of the game (win, loss, or draw) for all possible move sequences. This method breaks down the complex problem of evaluating all possible future moves into simpler, manageable steps, allowing the algorithm to explore potential outcomes systematically.

CHAPTER 4: THE POWER OF FUNCTIONS, MODULES, PACKAGES AND LAMBDAS

Although the MinMax algorithm might be considered overkill for a relatively simple game like Tic-Tac-Toe, it serves as an excellent educational tool. The principles behind MinMax are also applied in more complex games like chess, checkers, Stratego™, Connect Four™, Reversi (Othello™), and Gomoku, where the ability to anticipate and counteract an opponent's moves is crucial.

# A Word from the Author

*"No matter which field of work you want to go in, it is of great importance to learn at least one programming language."* — *Ram Ray*

I hope you're enjoying this journey into Python and starting to see its possibilities. If you're finding the content helpful or inspiring, I'd love to hear your thoughts. Your feedback is invaluable—it helps others discover Python and supports future learners.

**By leaving a short review on Amazon, you'll help others start their own Python adventure, and your review can make a real difference in someone else's journey.**

**Thank you for helping spread the knowledge!**

*Scan the following QR code…*

Amazon
Absolute Beginner's Guide to Python Programming
https://www.amazon.com/review/create-review/?asin=1964520002

# Chapter 5: Data Storage: Text & JSON Files

In this chapter, we will explore how to handle files in Python, focusing on working with text and JSON files. File handling is essential for any programmer because it allows applications to store and retrieve important data securely and efficiently.

Imagine you have a personal journal where you jot down your thoughts, experiences, and plans each day. This journal is precious to you because it holds all your important memories and information. Similarly, an application needs a place to store its important data, and that place is a file. When you write in your journal, you open it, write your entry, and then close it to keep your thoughts safe. Similarly, when an application needs to store data, it opens a file, writes it, and then closes it to ensure it is saved properly.

This process of opening, writing, and closing a file is what we call file handling in programming. By learning how to handle files in Python, you'll be able to create applications that can store and retrieve important information, just like writing and reading entries from a journal.

Throughout this chapter, we'll build a personal expense tracker. This project will help you understand file handling by providing a practical application. By the end, you'll be able to read, write, and manage expenses stored in various file formats, ensuring data is stored securely and efficiently.

Let's dive into the world of file handling in Python and see how we can store our data in a structured and organized manner.

## 5.1 Basic File Operations

To work with files in Python, you use the `open()` function, which returns a file object. This object provides methods and attributes to perform various operations on the file, such as reading or writing. After finishing your operations, it's essential to close the file using the `close()`

method to release the resources tied to the file and ensure that all your changes are properly saved to disk.

Here's how you can open and close a file in Python:

```
file = open('journal.txt', 'r')
# Perform file operations
file.close()
```

In this example, we open a file named `journal.txt` in read mode (`'r'`). After performing the desired operations, we close the file to ensure all resources are released properly.

However, this approach has a downside. If an error occurs between the `open()` and `close()` calls, there's a risk the file might not close properly. This is where the `with` statement becomes invaluable.

## Using the `with` Statement

The `with` statement simplifies file handling by automatically taking care of closing the file after completing the operations, even if an error occurs during the process. This makes your code cleaner and more reliable.

```
with open('journal.txt', 'r') as file:
    entries = file.read()
    print(entries)
```

In this example, the file is opened using the `with` statement, which ensures that the file is closed properly after the block of code is executed.

## File Modes for Opening Files

When opening files in Python, you need to specify the mode, which determines how the file will be accessed. Below is a table explaining the different file modes:

| Mode | Description |
| --- | --- |
| `'r'` | Read mode (default). Opens the file for reading. If the file does not exist, it raises a `FileNotFoundError`. |
| `'w'` | Write mode. Opens the file for writing. If the file exists, it truncates the file to zero length (erases its contents). If the file does not exist, it creates a new file. |
| `'a'` | Append mode. Opens the file for writing. If the file exists, the file pointer is placed at the end of the file, and new data is appended to the existing data. If the file does not exist, it creates a new file. |
| `'x'` | Exclusive creation mode. Creates a new file and raises a `FileExistsError` if the file already exists. |
| `'b'` | Binary mode. This is used in conjunction with other modes (`'r'`, `'w'`, or `'a'`) to open the file in binary mode, which is necessary for non-text files like images or executable files. |

## 5.2 File Paths and Directories

Before working with files, it's important to understand where your program is looking for files or writing them. By default, Python uses the current working directory for file operations unless you specify a different path. Let's explore how you can query the current working directory and specify a different directory for reading and writing files.

### Querying the Current Working Directory

The os module in Python provides a method called getcwd() that allows you to query the current working directory. This is useful when you want to verify where your program is operating.

```python
import os

# Get the current working directory
current_directory = os.getcwd()
print(f"Current working directory: {current_directory}")
```

### Specifying a File Path

Instead of relying on the default directory, you can specify the full path of the file. This gives you control over where the file is read from or written to.

```python
# Specify a file path
file_path = '/path/to/your/directory/journal.txt'

# Open the file using the specified path
with open(file_path, 'r') as file:
    entries = file.read()
    print(entries)
```

### Changing the Working Directory

You can change the current working directory using os.chdir(). This is useful if you want to switch to a different directory for all subsequent file operations.

```python
import os

# Change the working directory
os.chdir('/path/to/your/directory')

# Verify the change
print(f"Changed working directory to: {os.getcwd()}")
```

## 5.3 Using Paths Across Different Operating Systems

When specifying paths, it's important to consider the operating system you're working on. Windows uses backslashes (\) while Linux and macOS use forward slashes (/). To ensure compatibility across platforms, use the os.path module to construct file paths.

```
import os

# Construct a file path
file_path = os.path.join('folder', 'subfolder', 'file.txt')
print(f"File path: {file_path}")
```

## 5.4 Handling Errors with `try/except/finally`

Even with the `with` statement ensuring that files are properly closed, various errors can still occur during file operations. For instance, the file you are trying to read might not exist, or you might not have the necessary permissions to access it. Handling these errors is crucial to prevent your program from crashing unexpectedly.

Using `try/except/finally` blocks in file handling enables you to handle errors effectively. You can report errors back to the user, retry operations, log the errors for further investigation, and ensure any necessary cleanup is performed.

Let's start with an example that handles a `FileNotFoundError`, which occurs when the file you are trying to open does not exist.

```
try:
    with open('journal.txt', 'r') as file:
        entries = file.read()
        print(entries)
except FileNotFoundError:
    print("The file was not found.")
finally:
    print("Finished reading the file.")
```

The try block contains the code that might throw an exception in this example. The `except` block handles the specific `FileNotFoundError`, and the `finally` block contains code that will always run, regardless of whether an error occurred.

### Handling Multiple Exceptions

Sometimes, more than one type of error might occur within a block of code. For example, you might also encounter a `PermissionError` if you don't have the necessary permissions to read a file. Or you have been reading the file, just fine but then the server or network goes down while you are in the middle of reading it.

You can handle multiple exceptions by adding additional `except` blocks. For example:

```
with open('journal.txt', 'r') as file:
    entries = file.read()
    print(entries)
except FileNotFoundError:
    print("The file was not found.")
```

```
except PermissionError:
    print("You do not have permission to read this file.")
except Exception as e:
    print(f"An unexpected error occurred: {e}")
finally:
    print("Finished reading the file.")
```

In this example, we handle both `FileNotFoundError` and `PermissionError`. The generic `except Exception as e` block catches any other exceptions that might occur.

## How to Know Which Exceptions to Handle

Determining which exceptions to handle involves understanding the potential issues that could arise during file operations. Common exceptions include:

- `FileNotFoundError`: Raised when the file does not exist.
- `PermissionError`: Raised when you don't have the necessary permissions to access the file.
- `IOError`: A more general exception for input/output errors.

In this chapter, we are focused on file handling. But there can be other types of exceptions depending on what you are doing. You can refer to the official Python documentation for a complete list of built-in exceptions and their descriptions. Reading error messages during testing and development will help you identify specific exceptions your program should handle.

By anticipating these potential issues, you can write more robust code that handles errors gracefully and provides a better user experience.

The Python Standard Library
Built-in Exceptions
https://docs.python.org/3/library/exceptions.html

## 5.6 Working with Text Files

### Reading from Text Files

Python provides several methods to read from a text file. The `read()` method reads the entire file as a single string, `readline()` reads one line at a time, and `readlines()` reads the entire file into a list of lines.

```
try:
    with open('journal.txt', 'r') as file:
        entries = file.read()
        print(entries)
except FileNotFoundError:
```

## Chapter 5: Data Storage: Text & JSON Files

```
    print("The file was not found.")
except PermissionError:
    print("You do not have permission to read this file.")
except Exception as e:
    print(f"An unexpected error occurred: {e}")
finally:
    print("Finished reading the file.")
```

In this example, we read the entire content of `journal.txt` and print it.

## Writing to Text Files

To write to a text file, you use the `write()` method, which writes a string to the file. To append text to an existing file, you open the file in append mode (`'a'`).

```
try:
    with open('journal.txt', 'w') as file:
        file.write("2024-05-25: Learned about file handling in Python.\n")
except Exception as e:
    print(f"An error occurred: {e}")
finally:
    print("Finished writing to the file.")
```

In this example, we write a new entry to `journal.txt`.

```
try:
    with open('journal.txt', 'a') as file:
        file.write("2024-05-26: Practiced writing and reading files.\n")
except Exception as e:
    print(f"An error occurred: {e}")
finally:
    print("Finished appending to the file.")
```

In this example, we append a new entry to `journal.txt`.

## Best Practices for Working with Text Files

- **Read Files Efficiently**: When reading large files, consider reading them in chunks or using a loop to process each line to avoid memory issues.

    ```
    try:
        with open('journal.txt', 'r') as file:
            for line in file:
                print(line.strip())
    except FileNotFoundError:
        print("The file was not found.")
    except PermissionError:
        print("You do not have permission to read this file.")
    except Exception as e:
        print(f"An unexpected error occurred: {e}")
    ```

```
finally:
    print("Finished reading the file.")
```

You may have noticed the calling of `strip()` with this line:

```
print(line.strip())
```

The `strip()` method is used to remove any leading (spaces at the beginning) and trailing (spaces at the end) whitespace characters from a string. This includes spaces, tabs (\t), and newline characters (\n). If there are no leading or trailing whitespace characters, strip() will return the original string.

- **Write Files Safely**: Use the `'x'` mode to create a new file, which fails if the file already exists, preventing accidental overwriting of data.

```
try:
    with open('journal.txt', 'x') as file:
        file.write("New entry.\n")
except FileExistsError:
    print("The file already exists.")
except Exception as e:
    print(f"An error occurred: {e}")
finally:
    print("Finished writing to the file.")
```

## 5.7 Working with JSON Files

JSON (JavaScript Object Notation) is a lightweight data-interchange format that is easy for humans to read and write and easy for machines to parse (interpret or understand) and generate. JSON is built on two structures: a collection of name/value pairs (similar to a Python dictionary) and an ordered list of values (similar to a Python list).

### Reading JSON Files

To read JSON data from a file, you use the `json.load()` method parses JSON data into a Python dictionary or list.

```
import json

try:
    with open('expenses.json', 'r') as file:
        data = json.load(file)
        print(data)
except FileNotFoundError:
    print("The file was not found.")
except json.JSONDecodeError:
```

## Chapter 5: Data Storage: Text & JSON Files

```
    print("Error decoding JSON.")
except Exception as e:
    print(f"An unexpected error occurred: {e}")
finally:
    print("Finished reading the file.")
```

In this example, we read JSON data from `expenses.json` and print it, with error handling to manage potential issues.

### Writing JSON Files

To write data to a JSON file, you use the `json.dump()` method, which converts Python objects into JSON format and writes them to a file.

```
import json

expenses = [
    {"date": "2024-05-25", "amount": 50.75, "category": "Grocery", "description": "Weekly groceries"},
    {"date": "2024-05-26", "amount": 120.00, "category": "Utilities", "description": "Electricity bill"}
]

try:
    with open('expenses.json', 'w') as file:
        json.dump(expenses, file, indent=4)
except Exception as e:
    print(f"An error occurred: {e}")
finally:
    print("Finished writing to the file.")
```

In this example, we write a list of expense entries to `expenses.json`, with error handling in place.

### Manipulating JSON Data

You can easily add, update, and delete data in a JSON file by reading the data into a Python object, manipulating the object, and then writing it back to the file.

```
import json

try:
    with open('expenses.json', 'r') as file:
        expenses = json.load(file)
except FileNotFoundError:
    expenses = []
except json.JSONDecodeError:
    print("Error decoding JSON.")
    expenses = []
except Exception as e:
    print(f"An unexpected error occurred: {e}")
```

```python
new_expense = {"date": "2024-05-27",
               "amount": 75.20,
               "category": "Entertainment",
               "description": "Concert tickets"}

expenses.append(new_expense)

try:
    with open('expenses.json', 'w') as file:
        json.dump(expenses, file, indent=4)
except Exception as e:
    print(f"An error occurred: {e}")
finally:
    print("Finished updating the file.")
```

In this example, we add a new expense to the list and save it back to the JSON file, with error handling to manage potential issues.

## Best Practices for Working with JSON Files

- **Validate JSON Data**: Before processing JSON data, validate its structure to ensure it meets your application's requirements.

```python
import json

try:
    with open('expenses.json', 'r') as file:
        data = json.load(file)
        # Validate JSON structure
        if isinstance(data, list) and all(isinstance(item, dict) for item in data):
            print("Valid JSON structure")
        else:
            print("Invalid JSON structure")
except json.JSONDecodeError:
    print("Error decoding JSON.")
```

- **Pretty-Print JSON**: Use the indent parameter in json.dump() to write more readable JSON files.

```python
import json

expenses = [
    {"date": "2024-05-25",
     "amount": 50.75,
     "category": "Grocery",
     "description": "Weekly groceries"},
```

```
    {"date": "2024-05-26",
     "amount": 120.00,
     "category": "Utilities",
     "description": "Electricity bill"}
]

with open('expenses.json', 'w') as file:
    json.dump(expenses, file, indent=4)
```

- **Handle Missing Files Gracefully**: When loading JSON data, handle `FileNotFoundError` gracefully and provide a fallback mechanism.

```
import json

try:
    with open('expenses.json', 'r') as file:
        expenses = json.load(file)
except FileNotFoundError:
    print("File not found. Starting with an empty expense list.")
    expenses = []
```

## 5.8 Other Types of Structured Files

While Chapter 5 delves into the essentials of working with text and JSON files, it's important to recognize the wide array of structured file formats available beyond these. Each format, from XML to INI to YAML, serves its own niche in data storage, configuration, and exchange. These alternative file types are complemented by dedicated Python libraries and cater to diverse use cases.

Understanding these formats can significantly broaden your programming toolkit, whether you're managing complex data hierarchies, crafting readable configuration files, or ensuring compatibility across different programming environments. Your project's specific demands, including the need for data complexity, ease of human interaction, and integration within your chosen tech stack, should guide your choice of which to use. This section aims to demonstrate these other structured file formats, highlighting their unique characteristics and suggesting the appropriate Python libraries for working with each.

### CSV

CSV (Comma-Separated Values) files are a simple text format for storing tabular data. Each line of the file is a data record, and each record consists of one or more fields separated by commas. This format is widely supported by spreadsheets and databases, making it a universal standard for exchanging tabular data between different programs and applications. Python's built-in `csv` module provides functionality to read from and write to CSV files easily.

CSV File Example (`example.csv`):

```
Name,Age,City
Alice,30,New York
Bob,25,Los Angeles
```

```python
import csv

# Writing to a CSV file
with open('example.csv', mode='w', newline='') as file:
    writer = csv.writer(file)
    writer.writerow(['Name', 'Age', 'City'])
    writer.writerow(['Alice', 30, 'New York'])
    writer.writerow(['Bob', 25, 'Los Angeles'])

# Reading from a CSV file
with open('example.csv', mode='r') as file:
    reader = csv.reader(file)
    for row in reader:
        print(row)
```

# XML

XML (eXtensible Markup Language) is a markup language that defines a set of rules for encoding documents in a human-readable and machine-readable format. It is primarily used for the storage and transport of data. Unlike JSON, XML is more verbose and allows for a greater degree of structure and metadata, making it well-suited for complex data representations. Python provides several libraries for working with XML data, with `xml.etree.ElementTree` being one of the most commonly used. It offers a simple and efficient way to parse XML data, navigate through elements, and modify or create XML documents from scratch.

**XML File Example (`example.xml`):**

```
<root>
    <child>This is child 1</child>
    <child>This is child 2</child>
</root>
```

```python
import xml.etree.ElementTree as ET

# Creating an XML file
root = ET.Element("root")
child1 = ET.SubElement(root, "child")
child1.text = "This is child 1"
```

```
child2 = ET.SubElement(root, "child")
child2.text = "This is child 2"

tree = ET.ElementTree(root)
tree.write("example.xml")

# Reading an XML file
tree = ET.parse("example.xml")
root = tree.getroot()
for child in root:
    print(child.tag, child.text)
```

## INI Files

INI files are simple text files with a basic structure composed of sections, properties, and values. They are commonly used for configuration settings, due to their straightforward format and ease of editing. In Python, the `configparser` module is designed to manage configuration files in the INI format. It allows for reading, writing, and modifying INI files with an API that makes accessing configuration values simple. The module supports a structure where configuration files are divided into sections, each containing keys with associated values, making it ideal for application settings.

**INI File Example (`example.ini`):**

```
[DEFAULT]
ServerAliveInterval = 45
Compression = yes
CompressionLevel = 9

[bitbucket.org]
User = hg

[topsecret.server.com]
Port = 50022
ForwardX11 = no
```

```
import configparser

# Writing to an INI file
config = configparser.ConfigParser()
config['DEFAULT'] = {'ServerAliveInterval': '45',
                     'Compression': 'yes',
                     'CompressionLevel': '9'}
config['bitbucket.org'] = {'User': 'hg'}
config['topsecret.server.com'] = {'Port': '50022', 'ForwardX11': 'no'}

with open('example.ini', 'w') as configfile:
    config.write(configfile)

# Reading from an INI file
config = configparser.ConfigParser()
```

```
config.read('example.ini')
for section in config.sections():
    print(section, dict(config[section]))
```

## YAML

YAML (YAML Ain't Markup Language) is a human-readable data serialization standard, ideal for configuration files, input files for data processing, and more due to its readability and support for complex data structures. Unlike JSON and XML, YAML supports comments, making it more user-friendly for manual editing. In Python, the `PyYAML` library is typically used to parse and generate YAML files. It provides functionality similar to JSON's, allowing for easy conversion between YAML data and Python objects. YAML's ability to represent hierarchies of data makes it particularly useful for configurations that require nested structures.

**YAML File Example (`example.yaml`):**

```
name: Alice
age: 30
city: New York
```

```python
import yaml

# Writing to a YAML file
data = {
    'name': 'Alice',
    'age': 30,
    'city': 'New York'
}

with open('example.yaml', 'w') as file:
    yaml.dump(data, file)

# Reading from a YAML file
with open('example.yaml', 'r') as file:
    data = yaml.load(file, Loader=yaml.FullLoader)
    print(data)
```

## 5.9 Chapter Summary

In this chapter, you learned about file handling in Python, focusing on working with text and JSON files. We covered the basics of opening, reading, writing, and closing files using both manual methods and statements for better resource management. We also discussed error handling with `try`, `except`, and `finally` blocks to ensure robust file operations.

Additionally, you were introduced to JSON files, including reading from and writing to JSON, and manipulating JSON data for practical applications. The chapter concluded with a discussion of other types of structured files, such as CSV, XML, INI, and YAML, highlighting their use cases and associated Python libraries.

In the next chapter, we will dive into the world of object-oriented programming (OOP) in Python. You'll learn about classes, objects, inheritance, and other key concepts that will help you easily structure your programs and manage complex data.

## 5.10 Chapter Exercises

### Exercise 1: Reading from a Text File

**Description**: Write a Python script to read and print the content of a text file.

**Task**:

1. **Open the File**: Use the open() function to open a text file in read mode ('r'). Ensure to handle the file using a with statement for automatic closing.

2. **Read the Content**: Use the read() method to read the entire content of the file. Print the content to the console.

3. **Error Handling**: Handle potential exceptions such as FileNotFoundError and PermissionError.

### Exercise 2: Writing to a Text File

**Description**: Write a Python script to write a new entry to a text file.

**Task**:

1. **Open the File**: Use the `open()` function to open a text file in write mode (`'w'`).

2. **Write Content**: Use the `write()` method to add a string to the file.

3. **Error Handling**: Handle potential exceptions that might occur during file operations.

### Exercise 3: Appending to a Text File

**Description**: Write a Python script to append a new entry to an existing text file.

**Task**:

1. **Open the File**: Use the `open()` function to open a text file in append mode (`'a'`).

2. **Append Content**: Use the `write()` method to append a string to the file.

3. **Error Handling**: Handle potential exceptions that might occur during file operations.

## Exercise 4: Reading from a JSON File

**Description**: Write a Python script to read data from a JSON file and print it.

**Task**:

1. **Import JSON Module**

2. **Open the JSON File**: Use the `open()` function to open a JSON file in read mode (`'r'`).

3. **Read and Parse JSON Data**: Use the `json.load()` method to parse the JSON data into a Python dictionary or list and then print the parsed data.

4. **Error Handling**: Handle potential exceptions such as `FileNotFoundError` and `json.JSONDecodeError`.

## Exercise 5: Writing to a JSON File

**Description**: Write a Python script to write a list of dictionaries to a JSON file.

**Task**:

1. **Import JSON Module.**

2. **Prepare Data**: Create a list of dictionaries representing expenses.

3. **Open the JSON File**: Use the `open()` function to open a JSON file in write mode (`'w'`).

4. **Write JSON Data**: Use the `json.dump()` method to write the Python objects as JSON data to the file.

5. **Error Handling**: Handle potential exceptions during file operations.

## Exercise 6: Adding a New Expense to a JSON File

**Description**: Write a Python script to add a new expense entry to an existing JSON file.

**Task**:

1. **Import JSON Module.**

2. **Read Existing Data**: Use the `json.load()` method to read existing data from the JSON file. If the file does not exist, handle the exception and start with an empty list.

3. **Add New Entry**: Append a new dictionary to the list of expenses.

4. **Write Updated Data**: Use the `json.dump()` method to return the updated list to the JSON file.

5. **Error Handling**: Handle potential exceptions during file operations.

---

## 5.11 Chapter Project: Personal Expense Tracker

**Description:** Create a personal expense tracker that reads, writes, and manipulates expense data stored in JSON files.

**Task**:

1. **Define the Data Structure**: The expenses should be stored as a list of dictionaries, each dictionary containing `date`, `amount`, `category`, and `description` keys.

2. **Reading Data**: Write a function to read expenses from a JSON file. Handle `FileNotFoundError` gracefully by starting with an empty list if the file does not exist.

3. **Writing Data**: Write a function to write expenses to a JSON file. Ensure data is properly formatted with indentation for readability.

4. **Adding an Expense**: Implement a function to add a new expense to the list and update the JSON file.

5. **Viewing Expenses**: Implement a function to display all expenses in a readable format.

6. **Error Handling**: Ensure robust error handling for file operations and JSON data processing.

**Step-by-Step Guide**:

1. **Define the Data Structure**:

```
expenses = [
    {"date": "2024-05-25", "amount": 50.75, "category": "Grocery", "description": "Weekly groceries"},
    {"date": "2024-05-26", "amount": 120.00, "category": "Utilities", "description": "Electricity bill"}
]
```

2. **Reading Data**:

```
import json

def read_expenses(file_path):
    try:
        with open(file_path, 'r') as file:
            return json.load(file)
    except FileNotFoundError:
        return []
    except json.JSONDecodeError:
        print("Error decoding JSON.")
        return []
    except Exception as e:
        print(f"An unexpected error occurred: {e}")
        return []
```

3. **Writing Data**:

```
def write_expenses(file_path, expenses):
    try:
        with open(file_path, 'w') as file:
            json.dump(expenses, file, indent=4)
    except Exception as e:
        print(f"An error occurred: {e}")
```

4. **Adding an Expense**

```
def add_expense(file_path, new_expense):
    expenses = read_expenses(file_path)
    expenses.append(new_expense)
    write_expenses(file_path, expenses)
```

5. **Viewing Expenses**:

```
def view_expenses(file_path):
    expenses = read_expenses(file_path)
    for expense in expenses:
        print(f"Date: {expense['date']}, Amount: {expense['amount']}, Category: {expense['category']}, Description: {expense['description']}")
```

6. **Main Function to Test the Tracker**:

```
def main():
    file_path = 'expenses.json'
    while True:
        print("\n1. Add Expense\n2. View Expenses\n3. Exit")
        choice = input("Enter your choice: ")
```

```python
            if choice == '1':
                date = input("Enter date (YYYY-MM-DD): ")
                amount = float(input("Enter amount: "))
                category = input("Enter category: ")
                description = input("Enter description: ")
                new_expense = {
                            "date": date,
                            "amount": amount,
                            "category": category,
                            "description": description}
                add_expense(file_path, new_expense)
            elif choice == '2':
                view_expenses(file_path)
            elif choice == '3':
                break
            else:
                print("Invalid choice. Please try again.")

if __name__ == "__main__":
    main()
```

**Tips for Success**:

- **Clarity and Precision**: Ensure your prompts are clear and your variables are well-named.
- **Error Handling**: Implement robust error handling to make your program user-friendly.
- **Test Thoroughly**: Test your program with different inputs to ensure it works correctly under various conditions.

# Chapter 6: Navigating Object-Oriented Programming

When I first encountered Object-Oriented Programming (OOP), it was a frontier as uncharted and bewildering as outer space. Back then, OOP was the new kid on the programming block, and even the "so-called" experts were grappling with its concepts. And the examples they used to explain OOP were completely unrelatable to me. I frequently thought, "What does that have to do with the problems I needed to solve as a programmer?" I remember feeling like I was at the foot of an insurmountable peak, doubting I would ever understand it.

But then, something clicked. I realized that OOP doesn't just mimic the real world; it distills it into a language that computers—and humans—can understand with astonishing clarity.

Imagine looking at the world around you and seeing it as a collection of objects, each with its unique properties and behaviors. My bottle of water on the desk, the bookshelf filled with novels, the clock ticking away time—they all suddenly transformed into objects in my mind's programming model. This epiphany was my breakthrough moment with OOP. It wasn't about complicating things; it was about organizing the complexity of life into understandable, manageable pieces.

Encapsulation, the first OOP concept we'll explore, was my gateway into this new way of thinking. It's like recognizing that each object in your life has its own internal state and a set of

CHAPTER 6: NAVIGATING OBJECT-ORIENTED PROGRAMMING

actions it can perform, hidden away from the outside world yet functioning seamlessly as part of a bigger system. This simple yet powerful idea is just the beginning.

In this chapter, we'll embark on a journey together, viewing the world through the lens of OOP. This perspective brings programming closer to the natural order of things, making it more intuitive and, frankly, more aligned with how we experience life. My hope is not just to teach you the principles of OOP but to share the wonder of seeing the ordinary transform into the extraordinary through the power of object-oriented thinking.

Let's dive into this adventure, not just as learners and teachers but as explorers discovering a language that bridges our digital creations with the world around us. By the end of this chapter, you might just find yourself looking at your surroundings and marveling at the objects that make up your world, both tangible and conceptual.

*Let's see if OOP will "Rock Your World!" like it did mine.*

## 6.1 What are Classes and Objects?

Look around you. What do you see? Are you at a desk? Is there a computer on your desk? Is there a lamp? A pen? A plant? A couch? A dresser? These are all objects.

Let's focus on the lamp for a moment. How would you describe it? You might note its color, shape, or the type of light it emits. What is it capable of doing? Perhaps it turns on and off, adjusts brightness, or even changes colors. What is its input? Maybe a switch flip, a button press, or even a voice command. And its output? Light varies in intensity or color based on your input. How do you interact with it? Through physical actions or commands, right?

In programming, especially object-oriented programming (OOP), we use "classes" and "objects" to describe and interact with the components of our software, similar to how we interact with physical objects like the lamp on your desk.

A class can be thought of as a blueprint or a template. It defines the properties (like color, brightness level) and behaviors (like turning on/off, adjusting brightness) that its objects will have, much like a design for a lamp specifies its characteristics and functionalities.

On the other hand, an object is a specific instance of a class—like one particular lamp on your desk. While the class serves as the general concept or blueprint, the object is the realization of that concept, complete with actual values for its properties (e.g., a red lamp, currently turned off) and the ability to perform its behaviors (e.g., the lamp can be turned on to illuminate your room).

Imagine the class as the idea of a lamp, encompassing all the potential features and actions a lamp can have. When you actually buy a lamp and place it on your desk, that lamp becomes an object. It has specific characteristics defined by the lamp class, but it also has its unique traits (like its position on your desk, the specific light it provides, etc.).

This way of thinking allows programmers to create complex, interactive systems that are organized and understandable. By defining classes, we can create multiple objects from the same blueprint, each with its own unique properties and behaviors, just like having different lamps in various rooms of your house.

## 6.2 Define a Class

There are countless ways to define (or describe) a lamp in Python code. But here is a simple version that has two attributes to represent its color and state (on or off), and two methods to turn on and off the lamp.

```python
class Lamp:
    def __init__(self, color, is_on=False):
        self.color = color
        self.is_on = is_on

    def turn_on(self):
        self.is_on = True
        print(f"The {self.color} lamp is now on.")

    def turn_off(self):
        self.is_on = False
        print(f"The {self.color} lamp is now off.")
```

There are a few new things in this code, that requiring a bit of explanation:

- **Class Definition**: The keyword `class` followed by `Lamp` starts the definition of our class. `Lamp` is the name of our class, which acts as a blueprint for creating lamp objects.
- **`__init__` Method**: This is a special method in Python, called a constructor. It's automatically called when a new object of the `Lamp` class is created. The `self` parameter refers to the current instance of the class and is used to access variables that belong to the class. The `__init__` method initializes the new lamp object with two attributes:
- **`Color` Attribute**: This attribute stores the color of the lamp. It's set when the lamp object is created, allowing each lamp to have a different color.

- **`is_on` Attribute**: This boolean attribute stores whether the lamp is on or off. It's optional and defaults to `False` (off) if not specified when the lamp object is created.
- **`turn_on` Method**: This method changes the `is_on` attribute of the lamp object to `True` (indicating the lamp is on) and prints a message stating that the lamp is now on. Notice how it uses `self` to access and modify the attributes of the specific lamp object.
- **`turn_off` Method**: Similarly, this method sets the `is_on` attribute to `False` and prints a message indicating the lamp is now off.

## 6.3 Creating and Using Objects

With the `Lamp` class defined, you can now create and interact with lamp objects in your code. Here's how you might create a blue lamp and turn it on:

```
blue_lamp = Lamp("blue")
blue_lamp.turn_on()
```

This code snippet creates a new `Lamp` object called `blue_lamp` with the color "blue". It then calls the `turn_on` method for `blue_lamp`, which sets its `is_on` attribute to `True` and prints "The blue lamp is now on."

By defining classes like `Lamp`, programmers can create objects that encapsulate both data (properties or attributes) and functions (methods) related to specific entities, making code more organized, reusable, and easier to understand.

Understanding classes and objects is the first step into the vast and fascinating world of object-oriented programming. As we delve deeper, you'll see how these concepts help us to model real-world scenarios in software, making our programs more modular, flexible, and intuitive to work with.

## 6.4 Understanding Composition: Classes Within Classes

As we venture deeper into the realm of Object-Oriented Programming (OOP), we encounter powerful concepts that not only make our code more efficient but also mirror the intricacy and interconnectedness of the real world. One such concept is composition, a fundamental OOP principle where objects are used to build more complex structures. To illustrate this, let's explore a practical example involving a `Customer` class that incorporates an `Address` class.

### The Address Class

Imagine you're tasked with storing address information for customers. Instead of jumbling all the details together, you smartly decide to encapsulate address-related data within its own class:

```python
class Address:
    def __init__(self, street, city, state, postal_code):
        self.street = street
        self.city = city
        self.state = state
        self.postal_code = postal_code

    def update_address(self, street, city, state, postal_code):
        """Updates the address details."""
        self.street = street
        self.city = city
        self.state = state
        self.postal_code = postal_code
        print("Address updated successfully.")
```

This `Address` class is straightforward, holding attributes like `street`, `city`, `state`, and `postal_code`. It also features a method, `update_address`, for updating these details, showcasing encapsulation and method functionality.

## The Customer Class

Now, let's consider our `Customer` class. Customers, in addition to their name and email, have an address. Here's how we can compose a customer object that includes an address:

```python
class Customer:
    def __init__(self, name, email, address):
        """Initializes a customer with name, email, and address."""
        self.name = name
        self.email = email
        self.address = address  # This is an Address object

    def display_customer_info(self):
        """Displays the customer's information."""
        print(f"Name: {self.name}")
        print(f"Email: {self.email}")
        print("Address:")
        print(f"  Street: {self.address.street}")
        print(f"  City: {self.address.city}")
        print(f"  State: {self.address.state}")
        print(f"  Postal Code: {self.address.postal_code}")

    def update_address(self, street, city, state, postal_code):
        """Updates the customer's address."""
        self.address.update_address(street, city, state, postal_code)
```

In the `Customer` class, the `address` attribute demonstrates composition by holding an `Address` object. This design allows us to manage customer addresses efficiently, maintaining the integrity of our data by ensuring that address-related information is handled within its rightful context.

CHAPTER 6: NAVIGATING OBJECT-ORIENTED PROGRAMMING

## Bringing It All Together

Let's put our classes to work:

```python
# Create an Address object for our customer
customer_address = Address("123 Main St", "Anytown", "Anystate", "12345")

# Create a Customer object, incorporating the Address object
customer = Customer("John Doe", "johndoe@example.com", customer_address)

# Initially display the customer's information
customer.display_customer_info()

# Suppose the customer moves; we update the address
customer.update_address("456 Elm St", "Newtown", "Newstate", "67890")

# Display the updated information to reflect the new address
customer.display_customer_info()
```

This example beautifully demonstrates the power of composition in OOP. By encapsulating address details within its own class and integrating it into the `Customer` class, we achieve a clean, organized, and modular code structure. It highlights how real-world relationships and hierarchies can be effectively modeled in software, making our programs more intuitive and manageable.

## 6.5 Wrapping Up Encapsulation

As we've journeyed through the realms of classes and objects, and explored the lands of composition with our `Customer` and `Address` classes, we've subtly danced with the principle of encapsulation—one of the cornerstones of object-oriented programming. Encapsulation isn't just about grouping variables and methods together in a class; it's about safeguarding the inner workings of that class, creating a clear and safe interface for the rest of your program to interact with.

### The Essence of Encapsulation

- **Data Hiding**: At its heart, encapsulation is about data hiding. Just as a magician conceals the secrets behind their tricks, encapsulation hides the internal state of objects. This is not to deceive, but to protect. The `update_address` method within our `Address` class is a perfect example. It shields the direct manipulation of address attributes, ensuring data integrity and preventing unintended side effects.
- **Simplifying Complexity**: Encapsulation is our ally in the battle against complexity. By wrapping data and the methods that act on that data in a single package, we allow ourselves to think about higher-level problems without getting bogged down in the details. Our `Customer` and `Address` setup exemplifies this, showing how complex entities can be managed structured and comprehensibly.

- **Reusability and Modularity**: The beauty of encapsulation also lies in its promotion of reusability and modularity. The `Address` class we've crafted is not just a one-hit wonder for our `Customer` class. It stands ready to be reused wherever an address is needed, showcasing the modular design at its finest.

- **Maintenance and Evolution**: Encapsulated code is like a well-organized library. It's easier to maintain and adapt to new needs. Changes within the `Address` class remain concealed from the `Customer` as long as their interaction stays constant. This separation of concerns ensures our code can evolve without causing a cascade of alterations throughout the entire program.

Having grasped the powerful concept of encapsulation, it's time to venture forward. The next logical step in our object-oriented programming odyssey is to explore the equally vital principles of inheritance, polymorphism, and abstraction. Each of these builds upon our foundation, weaving a richer tapestry of understanding that will allow you to craft more sophisticated and efficient software.

## 6.6 Embracing Inheritance

Inheritance in OOP is akin to inheriting traits from our parents yet possessing unique characteristics. It allows one class, known as a subclass or child class, to inherit the attributes and methods of another class, referred to as a superclass or parent class. This principle fosters a natural organizational hierarchy within programming, enabling a more structured and intuitive design.

### Basic Syntax and Structure

In Python, inheriting from a class is straightforward. Suppose we define a basic class `Vehicle` that serves as our parent class. We can then create a `Car` class that inherits from `Vehicle`, adopting its attributes and methods while introducing some of its own.

```python
class Vehicle:
    def __init__(self, make, year):
        self.make = make
        self.year = year

    def start(self):
        print(f"The {self.make} vehicle is starting.")

class Car(Vehicle):  # Inherits from Vehicle
    def __init__(self, make, year, model):
        super().__init__(make, year)  # Call the parent class's constructor
        self.model = model

    def start(self):
        print(f"The {self.make} {self.model}, {self.year}, is starting.")
```

# Chapter 6: Navigating Object-Oriented Programming

## Key Concepts of Inheritance

- **Single Inheritance**: When a class inherits from only one parent class. Our `Car` class demonstrates single inheritance by deriving from the `Vehicle` class.

- **Multiple Inheritance**: Occurs when a class inherits from more than one parent class. This feature allows for a more flexible design but can introduce complexity.

```python
class ElectricVehicle:
    def charge(self):
        print("Charging the vehicle.")

class ElectricCar(Car, ElectricVehicle):  # Inherits from both Car and ElectricVehicle
    pass
```

- **Overriding Methods**: A subclass can provide its specific implementation of a method from the parent class. In our example, `Car` overrides the `start` method of `Vehicle`.

- **Super Function**: The `super()` function is used to call methods from the parent class. This is useful when extending or modifying the functionality of inherited methods, as shown in the `Car` constructor.

## Advantages of Using Inheritance

- **Code Reusability**: Inheritance encourages the reuse of code. The `Car` class can utilize the attributes and methods of `Vehicle` without redefining them.

- **Creating Hierarchies:** It helps establish clear, logical class hierarchies, simplifying the understanding and management of complex codebases.

- **Extensibility**: Inheritance facilitates the extension of existing code. New classes can be developed on top of existing structures, enhancing functionality without altering the foundational code.

## Practical Application of Inheritance

Consider developing a software system for a car rental service. We might have various types of vehicles, each sharing common features (like make and year) but also possessing specific attributes (like a model or charging capability for electric vehicles).

```python
# Define Vehicle, Car, and ElectricCar as shown above

# Create an instance of ElectricCar
tesla_model_s = ElectricCar("Tesla", 2020, "Model S")
tesla_model_s.charge()   # Specific to ElectricCar
tesla_model_s.start()    # Overridden method from Car, which inherits Vehicle's method
```

This hierarchy simplifies the representation of different vehicle types, allowing for shared and unique behaviors among them.

## 6.7 Wrapping up Inheritance

Inheritance is a cornerstone of OOP, enabling efficient code reuse, logical hierarchies, and easy extensibility. By understanding and applying inheritance, programmers can craft more organized, scalable, and maintainable codebases.

Next, we'll explore Polymorphism, another OOP principle that allows objects of different classes to be treated as objects of a common superclass, further enhancing the flexibility and functionality of our programs.

## 6.8 Exploring Polymorphism

Polymorphism, from the Greek words for "many shapes," is a concept in object-oriented programming (OOP) that allows objects of different classes to be treated as objects of a common superclass. It's the ability for different classes to respond to the same method call in different, yet related ways. Imagine a simple scenario: you, taking on different roles throughout the day—as an employee, a parent, or a passenger. Despite the different behaviors in each role, it's still you at the core. Similarly, polymorphism lets us perform a single action in different ways.

### Types of Polymorphism

**Compile-Time Polymorphism (Method Overloading):** This type of polymorphism occurs when multiple methods within a class have the same name but different parameters. For example, based on the arguments provided, a drawing method could be overloaded to draw various shapes, such as circles, rectangles, or triangles.

**Run-Time Polymorphism (Method Overriding):** This occurs when a subclass provides a specific implementation for a method that is already provided by its parent class. This way, the method behaves differently depending on the object that invokes it. For instance, a generic `Vehicle` class method `start()` could be overridden by `Car` and `Bike` subclasses to start a car or bike specifically.

### Implementing Polymorphism

With its dynamic typing, Python doesn't support traditional compile-time polymorphism (method overloading) as seen in statically typed languages. However, Python's flexibility allows for polymorphic behavior primarily through method overriding and duck typing.

Consider this example demonstrating run-time polymorphism:

```
class Vehicle:
    def start(self):
        print("Starting the vehicle")

class Car(Vehicle):
    def start(self):
```

## Chapter 6: Navigating Object-Oriented Programming

```
        print("Starting the car")

class Bike(Vehicle):
    def start(self):
        print("Starting the bike")

def start_vehicle(vehicle):
    vehicle.start()

# Creating instances
car = Car()
bike = Bike()

# Demonstrating polymorphism
start_vehicle(car)   # Output: Starting the car
start_vehicle(bike)  # Output: Starting the bike
```

In this example, the `start_vehicle` function uses the `start` method of whichever vehicle it's given, showcasing polymorphism by treating different objects as instances of their superclass `Vehicle`.

### Benefits of Polymorphism

- **Flexibility**: Polymorphism allows for the flexible use of a single interface, enabling the same method to be used for different purposes across various objects.

- **Simplicity**: It simplifies code management by reducing the need for long, complex conditional statements to determine an object's type before acting on it.

- **Maintainability**: Polymorphism enhances maintainability through loose coupling and minimizes dependencies, making it easier to extend and manage code.

### Practical Applications of Polymorphism

- **Graphic User Interface (GUI) Components**: In GUI development, polymorphism allows for the creation of a unified set of operations (like `draw` or `click`) that can be applied across various components (buttons, sliders, checkboxes), each with its unique behavior.

- **Payment Processing Systems:** Polymorphism simplifies the integration and management of various payment methods (credit cards, PayPal, cryptocurrencies) in a system by allowing them to be processed through a common interface, facilitating the easy addition of new payment methods.

## 6.9 Wrapping up Polymorphism

Polymorphism is a pivotal concept in OOP that grants programmers the ability to design flexible and dynamic systems. Polymorphism enhances code reusability, simplicity, and maintainability by treating objects of different classes similarly. As we've seen, its applications range from simplifying GUI component management to streamlining payment processing systems, underscoring its importance in efficient software design.

Moving forward, we will delve into Abstraction, another fundamental OOP principle. Abstraction complements polymorphism by allowing us to focus on what an object does instead of how it does it, further contributing to the robustness and clarity of our software designs.

## 6.10 Mastering Abstraction

Abstraction in software development is akin to focusing on what a car does—moving forward or backward—without needing to understand the intricacies of its engine or transmission systems. This principle of hiding complexity while revealing necessary functionalities is pivotal in Object-Oriented Programming (OOP). It allows developers to interact with objects at a higher level, ensuring that the underlying implementation details remain obscured.

### Principles of Abstraction

At its core, abstraction is about separating a system's purpose from its implementation, making it easier to understand and use. In OOP, this is achieved by defining classes that represent abstract concepts and entities. These classes expose methods and properties relevant to their role while the inner workings remain concealed, promoting a cleaner, more intuitive interface for developers.

### Implementing Abstraction in Python

Python achieves abstraction through abstract classes and interfaces, albeit in its unique, dynamically typed way.

- **Abstract Classes**: Python's ABC (Abstract Base Class) module provides the infrastructure for defining abstract classes. An abstract class can include one or more abstract methods, which are methods declared in the class but must be implemented by subclass(es).

```
from abc import ABC, abstractmethod

class Vehicle(ABC):
    @abstractmethod
    def start(self):
        pass

class Car(Vehicle):
    def start(self):
        print("Car starts with a key.")
```

In this example, `Vehicle` serves as an abstract class that defines a contract for its subclasses, like `Car`, ensuring they provide specific implementations for the `start` method.

- **Interfaces**: Python does not explicitly support interfaces, as seen in languages like Java. Instead, it leverages duck typing—"If it looks like a duck and quacks like a duck, it must be a duck"—allowing for a form of polymorphism where the exact type of an object is less important than the methods it defines.

## 6.11 Abstract Classes vs Interfaces

While Python's dynamic nature does not strictly enforce interfaces, the concept is implicitly supported. Abstract classes define a skeletal framework that subclasses must complete, potentially sharing some implementation. In contrast, interfaces (realized through duck typing) focus purely on method signatures, promoting even greater flexibility and decoupling between objects.

### Benefits of Abstraction

- **Simplification**: By exposing only the necessary parts of a system, abstraction makes complex systems easier to understand and use.
- **Flexibility**: It allows for changes in the implementation of an abstract interface without disrupting its users, promoting adaptable code.
- **Security**: Abstracting the internal workings of classes can prevent misuse and protect the integrity of the data and behavior.

### Practical Applications of Abstraction

- **Database Systems**: Abstraction is fundamental in database interaction, where complex queries are executed through simple method calls, hiding data connection details and manipulation.
- **API Development**: APIs are abstract interfaces to software or services, offering a simplified means of performing complex operations, whether it's sending data over the network or processing multimedia.

### Challenges and Considerations

Implementing abstraction comes with its challenges. Over-abstraction can lead to unnecessary complexity, potentially impacting performance and maintainability. It's essential to find the right balance, ensuring that abstraction simplifies development without introducing additional layers of complexity.

## 6.12 Wrapping up Abstraction

Abstraction is a cornerstone of OOP, essential for developing scalable, maintainable, and usable code. By focusing on "what" an object does rather than "how" it achieves it, abstraction lays the foundation for more complex principles like encapsulation, inheritance, and polymorphism.

## 6.13 The Bigger Picture: What OOP Really Unlocks

When I was first learning object-oriented programming, someone told me, "You just need to put on your OOP glasses." At the time, I thought they were joking. But they were right.

OOP isn't just a coding technique—it's a way of viewing the world. Once you learn to spot patterns like *"this thing has properties (or attributes) and functions (or methods) that do stuff,"* everyday life starts looking like a class diagram.

That coffee mug on your desk? It's an object. It has attributes—color, volume, temperature—and methods: fill(), sip(), wash().
Your dog? Also an object. Your calendar? Your to-do list? Same story.

By now, you've started building your own classes, attributes, and methods. That's the shallow end of the object-oriented programming pool. But don't be fooled—it goes *way* deeper.

As your skills grow, you'll explore the four core pillars of OOP:

- **Encapsulation**: bundling data and behavior together
- **Inheritance**: reusing code from one class in another
- **Polymorphism**: treating different objects the same way
- **Abstraction**: hiding complexity behind simple interfaces

You don't need to master all that today. But now you know it's out there.

And here's the best part: the tools you're using right now? They're the same ones used to build massive web apps, video games, AI systems, and more.
You're not just learning OOP—you're learning how to think like a programmer.

**And that's when OOP gets even more exciting.**
**Line upon line, step by step—you'll get there. You're building a life of learning, and the journey is just beginning.**

CHAPTER 6: NAVIGATING OBJECT-ORIENTED PROGRAMMING

## 6.14 Chapter Summary

In this chapter, we embarked on a journey through the core principles of Object-Oriented Programming (OOP), unraveling its transformative impact on software development. We began by exploring the concepts of classes and objects, where classes serve as blueprints defining the properties and behaviors of objects, and objects are instances of these classes, encapsulating specific data and functionality. Through practical examples, such as the `Lamp` class, we saw how to define attributes and methods, bringing abstract concepts to life.

We then delved into more advanced OOP principles, including encapsulation, inheritance, polymorphism, and abstraction. Encapsulation demonstrated the importance of bundling data and methods within a class, promoting data hiding and enhancing code modularity. The composition was illustrated with the `Customer` and `Address` classes, showcasing how complex objects can be constructed from simpler ones. Inheritance allowed us to see how a class can inherit attributes and methods from another, fostering code reuse and creating a natural hierarchy, as demonstrated with the `Vehicle` and `Car` classes. Polymorphism revealed how objects of different classes can be treated as objects of a common superclass, enhancing flexibility and simplicity in our code. Finally, abstraction highlighted the importance of exposing only the necessary parts of an object while hiding its implementation details, simplifying interaction, and enhancing security, as exemplified by the `Shape`, `Circle`, and `Rectangle` classes.

We built an enhanced expense tracker application through these concepts, integrating OOP principles to manage and manipulate expense data effectively. This project demonstrated the practical utility of OOP, emphasizing its role in creating organized, maintainable, and scalable software. With a solid foundation in OOP, you are now equipped to tackle more complex programming challenges, ready to design and implement sophisticated systems that mirror the complexity and elegance of the real world.

---

## 6.15 Chapter Exercises

### Exercise 1: Define and Use a Class

**Description**: Create a class to represent a book and instantiate objects of this class.

**Task**:

1. **Define the Class**: Define a `Book` class with title, author, and year attributes. Include an `__init__` method to initialize these attributes.

2. **Add Methods**: Add a method to display book details.

3. **Create Objects**: Create instances of the `Book` class and call the method to display their details.

## Exercise 2: Use Composition

**Description**: Create a `Library` class that contains multiple `Book` objects.

**Task**:

1. **Define the Library Class**: Define a `Library` class with an attribute for a list of books. Include an `__init__` method to initialize this list.

2. **Add Methods**: Add methods to add a book to the library and to display all books.

3. **Use Composition**: Create instances of the `Book` class and add them to the `library`.

## Exercise 3: Implement Inheritance

**Description**: Create a subclass `EBook` that inherits from `Book` and adds an attribute for file size.

**Task**:

1. **Define the Subclass**: Define an `EBook` class that inherits from `Book`. Add an attribute for file size and include it in the `__init__` method.

2. **Override Methods**: Override the `display_details` method to include file size.

3. **Create Objects**: Create instances of `EBook` and call the method to display their details.

## Exercise 4: Demonstrate Polymorphism

**Description**: Use polymorphism to handle different types of books with a common interface.

**Task**:

1. **Define a Function**: Define a function that accepts a book object and calls its `display_details` method.

2. **Create Objects**: Create instances of `Book` and `EBook`.

3. **Call the Function**: Pass the book objects to the function and observe polymorphism in action.

CHAPTER 6: NAVIGATING OBJECT-ORIENTED PROGRAMMING

## Exercise 5: Use Abstraction

**Description**: Create an abstract class `Shape` with abstract methods for calculating area and perimeter.

**Task**:

1. **Define the Abstract Class**: Use the `ABC` module to define an abstract class `Shape`. Add abstract methods `calculate_area` and `calculate_perimeter`.

2. **Create Subclasses**: Create subclasses `Circle` and `Rectangle` that inherit from `Shape`. Implement the abstract methods in each subclass.

3. **Create Objects**: Create instances of `Circle` and `Rectangle` and call their methods.

---

## 6.15 Chapter Project: Enhanced Expense Tracker with OOP

**Description:** Create a personal expense tracker that reads, writes, and manipulates expense data stored in JSON files using Object-Oriented Programming (OOP) principles.

**Task:**

1. **Define the Data Structure**: The expenses should be represented using an `Expense` class.

2. **Expense Management**: Implement an `ExpenseTracker` class to manage the collection of expenses.

3. **Reading Data**: Implement a method to read expenses from a JSON file.

4. **Writing Data**: Implement a method to write expenses to a JSON file.

5. **Adding an Expense**: Implement a method to add a new expense.

6. **Viewing Expenses**: Implement a method to display all expenses.

7. **Error Handling**: Ensure robust error handling for file operations and JSON data processing.

## 6.17 Step-by-Step Guide:

1. **Define the Expense Class**:

```python
class Expense:
    def __init__(self, date, amount, category, description):
        self.date = date
        self.amount = amount
        self.category = category
        self.description = description

    def __str__(self):
        return f"Date: {self.date}, Amount: {self.amount}, Category: {self.category}, Description: {self.description}"
```

## 2. **Define the ExpenseTracker Class**:

```python
import json

class ExpenseTracker:
    def __init__(self, file_path):
        self.file_path = file_path
        self.expenses = self.read_expenses()

    def read_expenses(self):
        try:
            with open(self.file_path, 'r') as file:
                expenses_data = json.load(file)
                return [Expense(**expense) for expense in expenses_data]
        except FileNotFoundError:
            return []
        except json.JSONDecodeError:
            print("Error decoding JSON.")
            return []
        except Exception as e:
            print(f"An unexpected error occurred: {e}")
            return []

    def write_expenses(self):
        try:
            with open(self.file_path, 'w') as file:
                json.dump([expense.__dict__ for expense in self.expenses], file, indent=4)
        except Exception as e:
            print(f"An error occurred: {e}")

    def add_expense(self, new_expense):
        self.expenses.append(new_expense)
        self.write_expenses()

    def view_expenses(self):
        for expense in self.expenses:
            print(expense)
```

## 3. **Update the Main Function to Use Classes**:

## Chapter 6: Navigating Object-Oriented Programming

```
def main():
    file_path = 'expenses.json'
    tracker = ExpenseTracker(file_path)

    while True:
        print("\n1. Add Expense\n2. View Expenses\n3. Exit")
        choice = input("Enter your choice: ")
        if choice == '1':
            date = input("Enter date (YYYY-MM-DD): ")
            amount = float(input("Enter amount: "))
            category = input("Enter category: ")
            description = input("Enter description: ")
            new_expense = Expense(date, amount, category, description)
            tracker.add_expense(new_expense)
        elif choice == '2':
            tracker.view_expenses()
        elif choice == '3':
            break
        else:
            print("Invalid choice. Please try again.")

if __name__ == "__main__":
    main()
```

## Tips for Success:

- **Clarity and Precision**: Ensure your prompts are clear and your variables are well-named.

- **Error Handling**: Implement robust error handling to make your program user-friendly.

- **Test Thoroughly**: Test your program with different inputs to ensure it works correctly under various conditions.

# CHAPTER 7: GRAPHICAL USER INTERFACES WITH TKINTER

After journeying through the essentials of Python and object-oriented programming, it's time to add another exciting tool to your toolkit: graphical user interfaces, or GUIs. With the Tkinter module, Python lets you create windows, buttons, and text fields, transforming your code into interactive applications.

Graphical User Interfaces (GUIs) make applications user-friendly by providing visual elements like buttons, text fields, and windows that users can interact with. Tkinter is Python's built-in library for creating GUIs. It is simple to use and comes bundled with Python, making it an excellent choice for beginners.

Tkinter is Python's standard GUI toolkit. It provides a fast and easy way to create GUI applications. Tkinter is lightweight and relatively easy to use compared to other GUI toolkits.

Tkinter is included in Python's standard library, so if you have Python installed, you can start using Tkinter without installing anything extra. It serves as a wrapper for the Tcl/Tk GUI toolkit, providing a Pythonic way to create and manage GUI elements.

Before diving into GUI programming with Tkinter, you need to ensure your environment is correctly set up.

CHAPTER 7: GRAPHICAL USER INTERFACES WITH TKINTER

## 7.1 Verifying Tkinter's Availability

Tkinter is included with Python as a standard library. To verify that Tkinter is installed and working, follow these steps:

1. **Create a New Python Script**:
    - Open your text editor or IDE.
    - Create a new Python file and name it something like `verify_tkinter.py`.

2. **Write the Verification Code**:
    - In the new file, write the following code:

    ```
    import tkinter

    tkinter._test()
    ```

3. **Run the File:** Save the file and run it using your text editor or IDE.

    You should see something like this:

    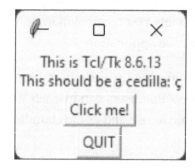

## 7.2 Troubleshooting Common Issues

- **tkinter Not Found**: If importing Tkinter results in a *ModuleNotFoundError*, your Python installation might not include Tkinter. This can happen with certain minimalist Python installations or operating systems. In this case, you might need to reinstall Python from the official website, ensuring you select the option to install Tkinter (usually included by default).

- **Updating Python**: If your Python version is outdated, download the latest version from python.org and install it. Modern Python installations include Tkinter by default.

- **Linux Users**: On some Linux distributions, Tkinter might not be included with the default Python package. You can usually install it via your package manager. For example, on Ubuntu, you can use `sudo apt-get install python3-tk`.

## 7.3 Your First Tkinter Application

Creating your first application with Tkinter is a milestone in your journey into GUI programming. This section will guide you through the process, starting with a simple window and gradually adding elements to make it interactive.

### Importing Tkinter

Every Tkinter application starts by importing the *tkinter* module. Open your favorite code editor or IDE, and let's begin by typing the following code:

```python
import tkinter as tk
```

### Creating the Main Window

The main window serves as the foundation for your application, where all other widgets (like buttons, labels, and text fields) will reside. Create the main window using the *tk.Tk()* class:

```python
root = tk.Tk()
root.title("My First Tkinter Application")
```

Here, *root* is a common convention for naming the main window object. It is the base or starting point of all graphical objects in your entire application, much like the root of a tree.

### Adding a Label and Button

Next, let's add a label and a button to the main window:

```python
label = tk.Label(root, text="Hello, Tkinter!", font=('Arial', 14))
label.pack(pady=10)

button = tk.Button(root, text="Click Me", command=on_button_click)
button.pack(pady=10)
```

Add the following function under the `import` statement:

```python
def on_button_click():
    label.config(text="Button clicked!")
```

### Starting the Event Loop

Finally, start the Tkinter event loop:

# Chapter 7: Graphical User Interfaces with Tkinter

```
root.mainloop()
```

This creates and starts a continuous loop that constantly checks for events and updates your GUI accordingly. Without it, your application would shut down immediately instead of waiting for user action.

Now, your code should look like this:

```
import tkinter as tk

def on_button_click():
    label.config(text="Button clicked!")

root = tk.Tk()
root.title("My First Tkinter Application")

label = tk.Label(root, text="Hello, Tkinter!", font=('Arial', 14))
label.pack(pady=10)

button = tk.Button(root, text="Click Me", command=on_button_click)
button.pack(pady=10)

root.mainloop()
```

Go ahead and run the code, You should see a window like the window on the left. And then when you click the button, "Hello, Tkinter!" turns into "Button clicked!"

*If you're like me, you are very emotionally "moved" by this first GUI program, which is working so beautifully. We can pause here for a moment to bask in the glory of what you've accomplished and allow you to get your composure....*

*You good? Awesome, let's continue. More awesomeness coming our way!*

*But as you wipe away your tears, you are probably asking yourself, "That's awesome. But how did I do it?"* Let's talk about that now:

**Explanation of the code:**

- **Importing Tkinter**: `import tkinter as tk` imports the Tkinter module and aliases it as `tk` for convenience.
- **Creating the Main Window**: `root = tk.Tk()` initializes the main window.
- **Setting the Window Title**: `root.title("My First Tkinter Application")` sets the title of the window.
- **Adding a Label**: `label = tk.Label(root, text="Hello, Tkinter!", font=('Arial', 14))` creates a label with specified text and font.
- **Adding the Label to the Window**: `label.pack(pady=10)` places the label in the window with padding.
- **Adding a Button**: `button = tk.Button(root, text="Click Me", command=on_button_click)` creates a button that calls `on_button_click` when clicked.
- **Adding the Button to the Window**: `button.pack(pady=10)` places the button in the window with padding.
- **Starting the Event Loop**: `root.mainloop()` starts the Tkinter event loop.

## 7.4 Layout Management

Labels and buttons are called widgets. Once you've created your widgets, you need to specify how they're arranged within the main window. This is where layout managers come into play. Tkinter provides several methods for this.

### Introduction to Layout Managers

Layout managers control the positioning and sizing of widgets within the main window. Tkinter provides three main layout managers: `pack()`, `grid()`, and `place()`.

### pack() Method

The `pack()` method in Tkinter arranges widgets in a block, where each block is stacked on top of or beside the others. In the example image, "Label 1" is positioned at the top of the window because it is the first widget packed with the `side="top"` option. This option specifies that the widget should be placed at the top of the available space, stacking vertically.

"Label 2" and "Label 3" are placed horizontally next to each other because they both use the `side="left"` option. This option specifies that the widgets should be placed to the left of the available space, stacking horizontally. The `fill="x"` option used with "Label 2" and "Label 3" allows these labels to expand horizontally to fill the available space.

Here is the example code that produces this layout:

```
import tkinter as tk

root = tk.Tk()
root.title("Pack Layout Example")

label1 = tk.Label(root, text="Label 1", bg="red", fg="white")
label2 = tk.Label(root, text="Label 2", bg="green", fg="white")
label3 = tk.Label(root, text="Label 3", bg="blue", fg="white")

label1.pack(side="top", fill="x")
label2.pack(side="left", fill="y")
label3.pack(side="left", fill="y")
```

**Explanation of the Code and Image:**

- **Label 1**: Packed with `side="top"`, so it is placed at the top of the window, occupying the full width (`fill="x"`).

- **Label 2**: Packed with `side="left"`, so it is placed to the left of the remaining space. It occupies the full height (`fill="y"`).

- **Label 3**: Also packed with `side="left"`, so it is placed to the right of "Label 2", occupying the full height (`fill="y"`).

This layout demonstrates how the `pack()` method can be used to create a simple yet structured arrangement of widgets in a Tkinter window.

## grid() Method

The `grid()` method in Tkinter places widgets into a grid of rows and columns, allowing for more complex layouts. Each widget is placed in a specific row and column, similar to a table structure. This method provides precise control over the positioning of widgets.

In the example image, "Label 1", "Label 2", and "Label 3" are arranged in a grid layout:

- "Label 1" is placed in the first row and first column (`row=0, column=0`).
- "Label 2" is placed in the second row and second column (`row=1, column=1`).

- "Label 3" is placed in the third row and third column (row=2, column=2).

Here is the example code that produces this layout:

```python
import tkinter as tk

root = tk.Tk()
root.title("Grid Layout Example")

label1 = tk.Label(root, text="Label 1", bg="red", fg="white")
label2 = tk.Label(root, text="Label 2", bg="green", fg="white")
label3 = tk.Label(root, text="Label 3", bg="blue", fg="white")

label1.grid(row=0, column=0)
label2.grid(row=1, column=1)
label3.grid(row=2, column=2)

root.mainloop()
```

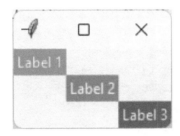

**Explanation of the Code and Image:**

Demonstrates the `grid()` method and how it arranges the widgets in a tabular.

- **Label 1**: Placed in the first row (row=0) and the first column (column=0). It appears at the top left corner of the grid.
- **Label 2**: Placed in the second row (row=1) and the second column (column=1). It appears in the middle of the grid.
- **Label 3**: Placed in the third row (row=2) and the third column (column=2). It appears at the bottom right corner of the grid.

This layout demonstrates how the `grid()` method can be used to create a structured and organized arrangement of widgets in a Tkinter window. Each widget is positioned based on its specified row and column, allowing for precise control over the layout.

## place() Method

The `place()` method in Tkinter allows you to explicitly set a widget's position and size using x and y coordinates. This method provides the most precise control over widget placement but requires you to manually manage the positions, which can be less flexible than the `pack()` and `grid()` methods.

In the example image, "Label 1", "Label 2", and "Label 3" are positioned at specific coordinates within the window:

- "Label 1" is placed at coordinates (50, 50).
- "Label 2" is placed at coordinates (100, 100).
- "Label 3" is placed at coordinates (150, 150).

Here is the example code that produces this layout:

```python
import tkinter as tk

root = tk.Tk()
root.title("Place Layout Example")

label1 = tk.Label(root, text="Label 1", bg="red", fg="white")
label2 = tk.Label(root, text="Label 2", bg="green", fg="white")
label3 = tk.Label(root, text="Label 3", bg="blue", fg="white")

label1.place(x=50, y=50)
label2.place(x=100, y=100)
label3.place(x=150, y=150)

root.mainloop()
```

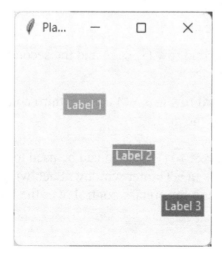

**Explanation of the Code and Image:**

- **Label 1**: Placed at coordinates (50, 50) using `label1.place(x=50, y=50)`. It appears 50 pixels from the left and 50 pixels from the top of the window.

- **Label 2**: Placed at coordinates (100, 100) using `label2.place(x=100, y=100)`. It appears 100 pixels from the left and 100 pixels from the top of the window.

- **Label 3**: Placed at coordinates (150, 150) using `label3.place(x=150, y=150)`. It appears 150 pixels from the left and 150 pixels from the top of the window.

This layout demonstrates how the `place()` method can be used to position widgets precisely within a Tkinter window. While this method provides exact control over widget placement, it requires more manual management and can be less adaptable to changes in the window size or content.

## 7.5 Choosing the Right Layout Manager

Choosing the right layout manager and understanding how to use it effectively is key to designing your GUI's structure:

- **pack()**: Best for simple, straightforward layouts. It's easy to use but less flexible.
- **grid()**: Ideal for more complex, grid-based layouts. It provides more control over widget placement.
- **place()**: Use when you need precise control over widget positioning. It's the most flexible but also the most difficult to manage.

## 7.6 Widgets: The Building Blocks of GUIs

Widgets are the elements that make up your GUI. They can be buttons, text fields, labels, sliders, and more. Each widget in Tkinter is represented as a Python object, and you'll add these to your main application window to create your interface. Widgets have properties (like text or size) and methods (like `pack()`, `grid()`, or `place()`) that you use to control their appearance and behavior.

### Labels

A Label widget displays text or images. It's one of the simplest yet essential widgets in Tkinter, often used to provide information to the user.

```
Example Code:
import tkinter as tk

root = tk.Tk()
root.title("Label Widget Example")
```

## CHAPTER 7: GRAPHICAL USER INTERFACES WITH TKINTER

```
label = tk.Label(root, text="This is a label", font=('Arial', 14), bg="yellow")
label.pack(pady=10)

root.mainloop()
```

**Explanation of the Code**:

- **Adding a Label**: `label = tk.Label(root, text="This is a label", font=('Arial', 14), bg="yellow")` creates a label with specified text, font, and background color.
- **Adding the Label to the Window**: `label.pack(pady=10)` places the label in the window with padding.

## Buttons

Buttons are interactive widgets that users can click to trigger actions. They are crucial for creating interactive applications.

```
import tkinter as tk

def button_click():
    print("Button clicked!")

root = tk.Tk()
root.title("Button Widget Example")

button = tk.Button(root, text="Click Me", command=button_click, bg="lightblue", font=('Arial', 14))
button.pack(pady=10)

root.mainloop()
```

**Explanation of the Code**:

- **Defining the Callback Function**: The `button_click` function prints a message when the button is clicked.
- **Adding a Button**: `button = tk.Button(root, text="Click Me", command=button_click, bg="lightblue", font=('Arial', 14))` creates a button with specified text, command, background color, and font.
- **Adding the Button to the Window**: `button.pack(pady=10)` places the button in the window with padding.

## Entry

An Entry widget allows users to input a single line of text. It's commonly used in forms and data input scenarios.

```python
import tkinter as tk

root = tk.Tk()
root.title("Entry Widget Example")

label = tk.Label(root, text="Enter your name:", font=('Arial', 14))
label.pack(pady=10)

entry = tk.Entry(root, width=30, font=('Arial', 14))
entry.pack(pady=10)

root.mainloop()
```

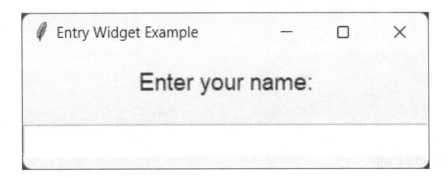

**Explanation of the Code**:

- **Adding a Label**: `label = tk.Label(root, text="Enter your name:", font=('Arial', 14))` creates a label with specified text and font.
- **Adding the Label to the Window**: `label.pack(pady=10)` places the label in the window with padding.

- **Adding an Entry**: `entry = tk.Entry(root, width=30, font=('Arial', 14))` creates an entry widget with specified width and font.
- **Adding the Entry to the Window**: `entry.pack(pady=10)` places the entry in the window with padding.

## Text

For multiline text input, the Text widget is your go-to. It provides a versatile area for user input, ideal for applications requiring more extensive data entry.

**Example Code**:

```
import tkinter as tk

root = tk.Tk()
root.title("Text Widget Example")

label = tk.Label(root, text="Enter your address:", font=('Arial', 14))
label.grid(row=0, column=0, padx=10, pady=10, sticky="e")

text_box = tk.Text(root, height=10, width=40, font=('Arial', 14), bg="lightyellow")
text_box.grid(row=0, column=1, padx=10, pady=10)

root.mainloop()
```

**Explanation of the Code**:

- **Adding a Label**: label = tk.Label(root, text="Enter your address:", font=('Arial', 14)) creates a label with specified text and font.
- **Adding the Label to the Window**: label.grid(row=0, column=0, padx=10, pady=10, sticky="e") places the label in the grid layout at row 0, column 0, with padding and aligns it to the right (east).

- **Adding a Text Box**: text_box = tk.Text(root, height=10, width=40, font=('Arial', 14), bg="lightyellow") creates a text widget with specified height, width, font, and background color.
- **Adding the Text Box to the Window**: text_box.grid(row=0, column=1, padx=10, pady=10) places the text box in the grid layout at row 0, column 1, with padding.

## Frame

A Frame is a container widget that holds and organizes other widgets. It's invaluable for complex GUI layouts, helping to group related elements together. In this example, we'll create a simple form with labels, entry fields, and a button inside a frame. When the button is pressed, an alert message will be displayed.

This example of the Frame widget contains a simple form with labels, entry fields, and a button. When the button is clicked, an alert message is displayed with the entered information.

```python
import tkinter as tk
from tkinter import messagebox

def submit_form():
    name = name_entry.get()
    email = email_entry.get()
    messagebox.showinfo("Form Submitted", f"Name: {name}\nEmail: {email}")

root = tk.Tk()
root.title("Frame Widget Example")

frame = tk.Frame(root, relief=tk.RAISED, borderwidth=2)
frame.pack(padx=10, pady=10)

name_label = tk.Label(frame, text="Name:", font=('Arial', 14))
name_label.grid(row=0, column=0, padx=5, pady=5, sticky="e")
name_entry = tk.Entry(frame, width=30, font=('Arial', 14))
name_entry.grid(row=0, column=1, padx=5, pady=5)

email_label = tk.Label(frame, text="Email:", font=('Arial', 14))
email_label.grid(row=1, column=0, padx=5, pady=5, sticky="e")
email_entry = tk.Entry(frame, width=30, font=('Arial', 14))
email_entry.grid(row=1, column=1, padx=5, pady=5)

submit_button = tk.Button(frame, text="Submit", command=submit_form, font=('Arial', 14))
submit_button.grid(row=2, column=0, columnspan=2, pady=10)

root.mainloop()
```

# Chapter 7: Graphical User Interfaces with Tkinter

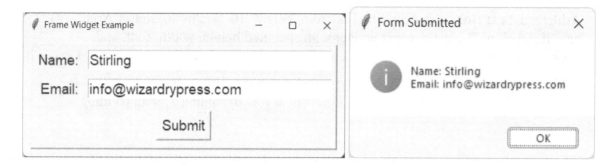

**Explanation of the Code**:

- **Adding a Frame**: `frame = tk.Frame(root, relief=tk.RAISED, borderwidth=2)` creates a frame with a raised relief and a border width of 2.

- **Adding the Frame to the Window**: `frame.pack(padx=10, pady=10)` places the frame in the window with padding.

- **Adding the Name Entry to the Frame**: `name_entry.grid(row=0, column=1, padx=5, pady=5)` places the entry in the grid layout at row 0, column 1, with padding.

- **Adding the Email Entry to the Frame**: `email_entry.grid(row=1, column=1, padx=5, pady=5)` places the entry in the grid layout at row 1, column 1, with padding.

- **Adding a Submit Button**: `submit_button = tk.Button(frame, text="Submit", command=submit_form, font=('Arial', 14))` creates a button that calls the `submit_form` function when clicked.

- **Adding the Submit Button to the Frame**: `submit_button.grid(row=2, column=0, columnspan=2, pady=10)` places the button in the grid layout at row 2, spanning both columns, with padding.

- **Defining the Callback Function**: The `submit_form` function retrieves the name and email from the entry fields and displays an alert message using `messagebox.showinfo`.

## 7.7 Message Boxes

Message boxes are a useful feature in Tkinter for displaying informational, warning, or error messages to the user. The `tkinter.messagebox` module provides several functions for creating different types of message boxes.

### Importing the Message Box Module

Before you can use message boxes in your Tkinter application, you need to import the `messagebox` module from `tkinter`:

```
from tkinter import messagebox
```

## Common Types of Message Boxes

Here are some common types of message boxes provided by the `messagebox` module:

- **showinfo**: Displays an informational message.
- **showwarning**: Displays a warning message.
- **showerror**: Displays an error message.
- **askquestion**: Displays a question dialog box with Yes/No options.
- **askokcancel**: Displays a dialog box with OK/Cancel options.
- **askyesno**: Displays a dialog box with Yes/No options.
- **askretrycancel**: Displays a dialog box with Retry/Cancel options.

## Parameters of Message Box Functions

Each message box function typically requires at least two parameters:

**Title**: The title of the message box window.

**Message**: The message text displayed in the message box.

Optional parameters include `icon` and `default` for customizing the appearance and behavior of the message box.

## Example: Displaying an Error Message

Here's an example of displaying a simple error message using the `showerror` function:

```
import tkinter as tk
from tkinter import messagebox

def show_error():
    messagebox.showerror("Error",
                    "Humor Not Found. Please check your joke settings.",
                    icon='error')

root = tk.Tk()
root.withdraw()   # Hide the root window

show_error()

root.mainloop()
```

# Chapter 7: Graphical User Interfaces with Tkinter

**Explanation**:

- **Importing Tkinter and Message Box**: `import tkinter as tk` and `from tkinter import messagebox` import Tkinter and the message box module.
- **Defining the Callback Function**: The `show_error` function displays an error message with a humorous twist and an error icon.
- **Hiding the Root Window**: `root.withdraw()` hides the root window since we only want to display the message box.
- **Starting the Event Loop**: `root.mainloop()` starts the Tkinter event loop.

## Asking a Yes/No Question

Here's an example of displaying a question dialog box using the `askyesno` function, including an icon and setting the default button:

```
import tkinter as tk
from tkinter import messagebox

def ask_yes_no():
    response = messagebox.askyesno("Confirmation", "Do you want to proceed?", icon='question', default='no')
    if response:
        messagebox.showinfo("Response", "You chose Yes!")
    else:
        messagebox.showinfo("Response", "You chose No!")

root = tk.Tk()
root.withdraw()   # Hide the root window

ask_yes_no()

root.mainloop()
```

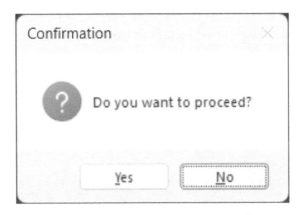

**Explanation**:

- **Defining the Callback Function**: The `ask_yes_no` function displays a yes/no question dialog with a question icon and sets the default button to 'No'.
- **Displaying Follow-Up Message**: A follow-up message is displayed using showinfo based on the user's response.
- **Hiding the Root Window**: `root.withdraw()` hides the root window since we only want to display the message box in our example code.

These examples demonstrate the basic usage of the `messagebox` module to display error messages and ask yes/no questions, including the use of icons and default button settings, while keeping the code simple to focus on the message box functionality.

## 7.8 Event Handling in Tkinter

Event handling is a fundamental aspect of GUI programming. It enables your applications to respond to user actions such as clicks, typing, or mouse movements. In Tkinter, this interaction is managed through event bindings and callbacks. This section will guide you through the basics of event handling in Tkinter, demonstrating how to make your applications interactive and dynamic.

### What are Events?

An event is any action or occurrence recognized by the program, such as pressing a key or moving the mouse. A binding is a connection between an event and a callback function: when the specified event occurs, the linked callback function is executed.

## Binding Events to Widgets

Most commonly, you'll bind events to widgets. For instance, you can bind a function to a button's click event.

```python
def on_click(event=None):
    label.config(text="Button was clicked!")

button = tk.Button(root, text="Click Me")
button.pack()

button.bind("<Button-1>", on_click)  # Bind left mouse click to on_click
```

## Handling Keyboard Events

Tkinter can also respond to keyboard events, allowing you to trigger actions based on the keys pressed by the user.

```python
def on_keypress(event):
    label.config(text=f"You pressed {event.char}")

root.bind("<Key>", on_keypress)  # Bind all key presses to on_keypress
```

This code makes the entire window listen for key presses and updates the label with the character of the pressed key.

## Using Lambda Functions for Parameters

Sometimes, you might want to pass additional parameters to your callback function. This can be achieved using lambda functions, enabling you to include extra arguments when the event is triggered.

```python
button = tk.Button(root, text="Click Me")
button.pack()

button.bind("<Button-1>", lambda event, arg="Extra Info": on_click(event, arg))
```

## 7.9 Event Sequences and Modifiers

Tkinter supports a variety of event sequences and modifiers, allowing you to create complex event bindings. For example, you can specify events for different mouse buttons, key combinations, and more.

```python
root.bind("<Control-c>", on_copy)  # Bind Control+c to on_copy function
```

## 7.10 Advanced Widget Customization and Styles

After grasping the fundamentals of Tkinter widgets and mastering event handling, the next step in refining your GUI applications involves advanced widget customization and applying styles. This section delves into enhancing your Tkinter widgets' visual appeal and functionality, making your applications functional and visually engaging.

### Customizing Widget Appearance

Each Tkinter widget comes with a set of options that allow you to customize its appearance and behavior. These options can be set through keyword arguments at the time of widget creation or dynamically modified with methods during runtime.

- **Colors**: Customize the background (bg) and foreground (fg) colors to enhance the visual layout of your widgets.

  ```
  button = tk.Button(root, text="Click Me", bg="blue", fg="white")
  button.pack()
  ```

- **Fonts**: The font option allows you to adjust the font type, size, and style to make the text in labels, buttons, and entries more readable or visually pleasing.

  ```
  label = tk.Label(root, text="Welcome", font=("Arial", 12, "bold"))
  label.pack()
  ```

- **Dimensions**: Control the size of widgets through height and width options, and manage the space around widgets using `padx` and `pady` for internal padding and `ipadx` and `ipady` for external padding.

## 7.11 Using ttk (Themed Tk) for a Modern Look

Tkinter includes a themed widget set known as ttk, which stands for Themed Tk. ttk provides access to more modern-looking widgets and allows for even finer control over the appearance of your applications through themes and styles.

- **Themes**: A theme is a set of visual styles that define the appearance of widgets. You can switch the overall theme of your application with *style.theme_use("theme_name")*.

- **Styles**: Create and apply custom styles to individual widgets or types of widgets.

  ```
  from tkinter import ttk
  style = ttk.Style()
  style.theme_use("clam") # Using a predefined theme
  #Creating a custom style for buttons style.configure("C.TButton", font=("Arial", 10), padding=10)
  #Applying the custom style to a button button = ttk.Button(root, text="Styled Button", style="C.TButton") button.pack()
  ```

## 7.12 Dynamic Widget Updates

Beyond static customization, Tkinter allows for dynamic updates to widgets, enabling your applications to respond to events with visual feedback. For example, you can change the text of a label in response to a button click or update the background color of a widget to indicate a state change.

```
def update_label():
    label.config(text="Updated Text", fg="green")

button = tk.Button(root, text="Update Label", command=update_label)
button.pack()
```

## 7.13 Integrating External Data and Services in Tkinter Applications

Beyond designing interactive and visually appealing interfaces, the real power of GUI applications often lies in their ability to interact with external data sources and services. This capability transforms a static interface into a dynamic and functional application. In this section, we'll explore how to enhance your Tkinter applications by fetching data from external APIs, reading from and writing to files, and integrating other external services and databases.

### Fetching Data from APIs

Interacting with web APIs is a common requirement for modern applications, enabling them to access real-time data such as weather updates, financial information, shipping status, or social media feeds.

- **Choosing a Python HTTP Client**: To make HTTP requests to an API, you can use Python's *requests* library, which simplifies sending HTTP requests and handling responses.

```
import requests

def fetch_weather_data(city_name):
    api_url = f"http://api.weatherapi.com/v1/current.json?key=YOUR_API_KEY&q={city_name}"
response = requests.get(api_url)
    if response.status_code == 200:
        return response.json()  # Parse JSON data from the response
    else:
        return None
```

- **Integrating API Calls into Tkinter**: Use the data fetched from APIs to update your GUI elements dynamically.

```
def update_weather():
    city = city_entry.get()
    data = fetch_weather_data(city)
    if data:
        weather_label.config(text=f"{city}: {data['current']['temp_c']}°C")
    else:
        weather_label.config(text="Data not found.")
```

## Reading and Writing Files

Many applications require reading from and writing to files for data persistence. Python's built-in file-handling functions work seamlessly within Tkinter applications.

- **Reading from a File**: Display content from a text file in a Tkinter Text widget.

```
def load_file_content():
    with open('example.txt', 'r') as file:
        content = file.read()
        text_widget.insert(tk.END, content)
```

- **Writing to a File**: Save content from a Tkinter Entry or Text widget to a file.

```
def save_content_to_file():
    content = text_widget.get("1.0", tk.END)
    with open('output.txt', 'w') as file:
        file.write(content)
```

## Integrating with Databases

Integrating a database can provide structured data storage and retrieval for applications requiring more complex data management.

- **SQLite Database**: Python's *sqlite3* module allows you to interact with SQLite databases directly, ideal for local data storage.

```
import sqlite3

def create_db():
    conn = sqlite3.connect('my_app.db')
    c = conn.cursor()
    c.execute('''CREATE TABLE IF NOT EXISTS users (username text, age integer)''')
    conn.commit()
    conn.close()
```

- **CRUD Operations**: Implement functions to create, read, update, and delete records in your database.

```python
def insert_user(username, age):
    conn = sqlite3.connect('my_app.db')
    c = conn.cursor()
    c.execute("INSERT INTO users VALUES (?, ?)", (username, age))
    conn.commit()
    conn.close()
```

Integrating external data and services into your Tkinter applications opens up endless possibilities for creating rich and interactive applications.

Whether it's fetching live data from web APIs, storing user input in files, or managing data with databases, these integrations make your applications more dynamic and useful. Experiment with these concepts and consider how they can enhance your projects' functionality and user experience.

## 7.14 Deploying Tkinter Applications: Best Practices and Sharing with Users

After developing your Tkinter application and integrating it with external data and services, the next crucial step is deployment. Deployment involves packaging your application into a format that can be easily distributed and run on users' machines, regardless of their operating system. This section will cover best practices for deploying tkinter applications and ensuring they are accessible and usable to your target audience.

### Creating a Standalone Executable

One of the most user-friendly ways to distribute a Tkinter application is by converting it into a standalone executable. This process packages your application with a Python interpreter and all the necessary modules, so users don't need to install Python to run your application.

- **Using PyInstaller**: PyInstaller is a popular tool for creating executables from Python applications for Windows, macOS, and Linux. It analyzes your Python programs to discover every other module and library your program needs to run. Then, it collects copies of all those files — including the active Python interpreter! — and puts them with your script in a single folder or, optionally, in a single executable file.

```
pip install pyinstaller
pyinstaller --onefile your_script.py
```

The `--onefile` flag tells PyInstaller to bundle everything into a single executable. After running this command, you'll find the executable in the dist directory.

## Testing Across Different Environments

Before distributing your application, testing it across different operating systems and environments is essential. This ensures compatibility and identifies any platform-specific issues that may need to be addressed.

**Virtual Machines and Containers**: Virtual machines (VMs) or containers can effectively test your application in clean, controlled environments that mimic different operating systems.

## Managing Dependencies

If your application relies on external libraries or modules, managing these dependencies is crucial for ensuring your application runs smoothly on other machines.

- **Requirements File**: Create a *requirements.txt* file listing all the external modules on which your application depends. This file can be used with pip to easily install all the necessary dependencies.

```
pip freeze > requirements.txt
```

## User Documentation

Providing clear, concise documentation is vital for helping users understand how to install and use your application.

- **Installation Instructions**: Include step-by-step instructions for installing your application, covering different operating systems as necessary.
- **User Guide**: Create a simple guide or manual that explains how to use your application, highlighting its features and functionalities.

## Updates and Maintenance

Finally, think about how you will manage updates and maintenance for your application.

- **Versioning**: Adopt a sensible versioning scheme (e.g., Semantic Versioning) for your application to help users and developers track changes and updates.
- **Update Mechanism**: Consider implementing an update mechanism within your application that automatically checks for and installs updates, improving the user experience.

Deploying a Tkinter application involves more than just packaging your code; it requires careful consideration of the end-user experience, from installation to daily use. By following best practices for creating standalone executables, managing dependencies, testing across

## 7.15 Chapter Summary

This chapter covered the basics of creating graphical user interfaces using Tkinter. We learned how to set up a simple Tkinter application, create and layout widgets, handle events, and integrate the game logic of a Tic-Tac-Toe game into a GUI application. By refactoring our console-based Tic-Tac-Toe game to a GUI version, we made the game more interactive and user-friendly, demonstrating the power and simplicity of Tkinter for Python GUI development.

---

## 7.16 Suggested Exercises

### Exercise 1: Create a Simple Calculator

**Description**: Create a simple GUI-based calculator that can perform basic arithmetic operations (addition, subtraction, multiplication, division).

**Task**:

1. **Set Up the GUI**: Create a main window using Tkinter. Add an `Entry` widget at the top to display the input and results.

2. **Create Buttons**: Create buttons for digits (`0-9`), arithmetic operations (`+`, `-`, `*`, `/`), and additional buttons for `=` and `C` (clear). Arrange these buttons in a grid layout for a calculator-like appearance.

3. **Define Button Actions**: When a digit or operation button is pressed, append its value to the `Entry` widget. When the `=` button is pressed, evaluate the expression entered in the `Entry` widget. Use Python's `eval` function to perform the calculation, but handle any errors that might occur. When the `C` button is pressed, clear the content of the `Entry` widget.

4. **Run the Event Loop**: Start the Tkinter event loop to make the GUI responsive.

**Hints**:

- Use the `grid` layout manager to position the buttons in a grid pattern.
- The `eval` function can evaluate a string expression but ensure that exceptions are handled using `try-except`.

- Use a callback function for each button's `command` to update the `Entry` widget.

**Partial Code Snippet**:

```python
import tkinter as tk

def evaluate_expression(expression):
    try:
        result = eval(expression)
        return result
    except Exception as e:
        return "Error"

def on_button_click(char):
    if char == "=":
        result = evaluate_expression(entry.get())
        entry.delete(0, tk.END)
        entry.insert(tk.END, str(result))
    elif char == "C":
        entry.delete(0, tk.END)
    else:
        entry.insert(tk.END, char)

# Set up main window, entry widget, and buttons here...
```

## Exercise 2: Create a To-Do List Application

**Description**: Create a GUI-based to-do list application where users can add, delete, and view tasks.

**Task**:

1. **Set Up the GUI**: Create a main window using Tkinter. Add an `Entry` widget for the user to input new tasks.

2. **Create a Listbox**: Add a `Listbox` widget to display the list of tasks. Add a scrollbar to the `Listbox` for better navigation when there are many tasks.

3. **Add Buttons for Actions**: Create an "Add Task" button that adds the text from the `Entry` widget to the `Listbox`. Create a "Delete Task" button that removes the selected task from the `Listbox`.

4. **Define Button Actions**: For the "Add Task" button, retrieve the text from the `Entry` widget, and add it to the `Listbox`. For the "Delete Task" button, remove the selected item from the `Listbox`. Ensure that an item is selected before attempting to delete.

5. **Run the Event Loop**: Start the Tkinter event loop to make the GUI responsive.

CHAPTER 7: GRAPHICAL USER INTERFACES WITH TKINTER

**Hints**:

- Use the `pack` or `grid` layout manager to organize the widgets.
- The `Listbox` widget's `insert` and `delete` methods can be used to add and remove tasks.
- Use `messagebox.showwarning` to alert the user if they try to add an empty task or delete without selecting a task.

```
import tkinter as tk
from tkinter import messagebox

def add_task():
    task = entry.get()
    if task != "":
        tasks_listbox.insert(tk.END, task)
        entry.delete(0, tk.END)
    else:
        messagebox.showwarning("Warning", "You must enter a task.")

def delete_task():
    try:
        task_index = tasks_listbox.curselection()[0]
        tasks_listbox.delete(task_index)
    except:
        messagebox.showwarning("Warning", "You must select a task to delete.")

# Set up main window, entry widget, listbox, and buttons here...
```

## 7.17 Chapter Project – Convert Tic-Tac-Toe to Tkinter

This project will guide you through converting the previously developed console Tic-Tac-Toe game into an interactive graphical user interface (GUI) version using Tkinter. By the end of this project, you will have a fully functional Tic-Tac-Toe game that users can play with clicks instead of console input, deepening your understanding of event-driven programming and GUI development in Python.

In Chapter 4, we completed a fully functional console-based version of our Tic-Tac-Toe game, which will serve as our foundation for transitioning into the GUI version of this project.

To kickstart your development with the GUI version, you can load the console game's code into your IDE. Alternatively, if you prefer a clean slate or need a refresher, you can start with the code provided in this book.

## 7.18 Designing the Tic-Tac-Toe GUI

In this section, we will design the graphical user interface (GUI) for our Tic-Tac-Toe game using Tkinter. Transitioning from the console to a GUI allows us to create a more engaging and interactive experience for the players. The design process involves planning the layout, choosing the appropriate widgets for game elements, and considering the user experience.

### Game Window and Layout

The first step in designing our GUI is to conceptualize the game window. This window will serve as the canvas for our game board, status messages, and control buttons. Our objective is to create a simple yet intuitive interface that enhances player interaction without overwhelming them with unnecessary complexity.

- **Window Size**: Decide on a fixed size for the game window to ensure that the layout remains consistent across different screen sizes. A window size of 300x300 pixels is sufficient to accommodate a 3x3 game board while leaving space for status messages and control buttons.
- **Title**: The window should have a descriptive title, such as "Tic-Tac-Toe," to identify the game to users clearly.

### Widgets for Game Elements

Tkinter offers a variety of widgets that we can use to build our game interface. Each widget serves a specific purpose, from displaying text to capturing user inputs. For our Tic-Tac-Toe game, we will use the following widgets:

- **Buttons**: The core of our game board will be represented by a grid of buttons. Each button corresponds to a cell on the Tic-Tac-Toe board. Players will make their moves by clicking these buttons. Initially, all buttons will be blank, and as the game progresses, they will display an 'X' or 'O', depending on the player's move.
- **Labels**: We will use labels to display important game status information. This includes messages indicating the player's turn (Player X or Player O), announcing the winner, or declaring a draw. Placing a label at the top or bottom of the game window ensures that the messages are clearly visible to both players.

### Planning the Layout

Tkinter's layout managers (pack, grid, and place) offer different ways to arrange the widgets. The grid layout manager is the most suitable option for our Tic-Tac-Toe game because it allows us to position widgets in a table-like structure, which is perfect for creating the game board.

- **Grid Layout**: Use the grid layout to arrange the buttons in a 3x3 matrix corresponding to the Tic-Tac-Toe board. The grid layout makes placing the buttons in specific rows and columns easy and provides the visual structure our game requires.

- **Control Panel**: Allocate space beneath the game board for a control panel that houses the "new game" and "quit" buttons. These buttons will enable players to start a new game or quit the application.

- **Status Display**: Allocate a section of the window, either above the game board or in the control panel, for the status label. This label will dynamically update to reflect the current game status, providing feedback to the players.

## User Experience Considerations

In designing the Tic-Tac-Toe GUI, our goal is to create a user-friendly and visually appealing game that invites players into the classic world of Tic-Tac-Toe with a modern twist. By thoughtfully arranging the game elements and considering the player's interaction, we can provide an enjoyable and seamless gaming experience.

- **Responsive Design**: Ensure that the buttons and text are large enough to be easily interacted with and read on various devices. While our window size is fixed, the design should remain accessible and user-friendly.

- **Feedback**: The interface should provide immediate visual feedback for player actions. For example, when a player clicks a button to mark a cell, the 'X' or 'O' should appear instantly to indicate the move.

- **Aesthetics**: While functionality is paramount, adding simple stylistic touches can greatly enhance the gaming experience. Consider using colors to differentiate between Player X and Player O's moves or to highlight the winning combination.

## 7.19 Review of Console Application

Before transitioning from console to GUI, let's revisit our console-based Tic-Tac-Toe from Chapter 4. This version established our game's fundamental mechanics and AI, which will integrate seamlessly into the new GUI, highlighting the value of our well-structured code. Notably, our focus will not include *main.py* or *game_ui.py*. Why is that? That's because they cater to a console-based application.

Let's explore the benefits of modularization and separation of concerns.

### Modifying the Game UI

First, let's create the game window and the grid for the Tic-Tac-Toe board. Tkinter makes this straightforward, allowing us to focus on the game's look and feel.

**Creating the Game Window**: Create a new module called *game_gui.py*.

Start by importing Tkinter and setting up your main application window. This window will serve as the foundation for your game's GUI.

```
import tkinter as tk

root = tk.Tk()
root.title('Tic-Tac-Toe')
```

**Setting Up the Grid**: The Tic-Tac-Toe board is essentially a 3x3 grid. We'll use buttons to represent each cell on the grid. When a player clicks a button, it'll mark an 'X' or 'O' in the cell.

Here's how to create the grid without using lambda for simplicity:

```
def create_button(row, col):
    def button_action():
        button_click(row, col)
    return tk.Button(root, text=' ', width=10, height=3, command=button_action)

for row in range(3):
    for col in range(3):
        button = create_button(row, col)
        button.grid(row=row, column=col)
```

In this setup, *button_click* is a function you'll define to handle the game's logic when a cell is clicked.

**Adding Status Messages**: Use Tkinter's Label widget to display messages like whose turn it is or who won the game. Place this label at the top or bottom of the window.

```
status_label = tk.Label(root, text="Player X's Turn", font=('Helvetica', 12))
status_label.pack(side="top")
```

## 7.20 Updating the Main File - Initializing the Tkinter Loop

In *main.py*, the newly created file for our GUI version, we start the Tkinter loop. This loop keeps the application running, waiting for user actions like button clicks.

```
if __name__ == '__main__':
    root.mainloop()
```

### Tying Together UI and Game Logic

The *main.py* file plays a crucial role in our application. It connects the visual interface we've just created with the underlying game mechanics and AI logic. This integration ensures that when a player interacts with the GUI, the game responds accordingly, providing a complete and functional game experience.

# CHAPTER 7: GRAPHICAL USER INTERFACES WITH TKINTER

Make sure the *button_click* function you used in creating buttons interacts correctly with the *game_mechanics.py* to update the game state.

Update the *status_label* text to reflect changes in the game state, such as turns and wins.

**The Importance of main.py**: *main.py* is where everything comes together. It initiates the GUI, responds to user inputs, and updates the game state and UI in response. It's a testament to how different components of our application—user interface, game logic, and AI—can work together harmoniously to create an engaging Tic-Tac-Toe game.

## 7.21 Step-by-Step Instructions

1. **Setting Up the Project**

    Create a new file: Name it *game_gui.py*.

    Import Tkinter: Add the necessary imports for Tkinter and other modules.

    ```python
    import tkinter as tk
    from tkinter import messagebox
    from game_mechanics import check_winner,
                               check_draw,
                               initialize_board,
                               X_PLAYER,
                               O_PLAYER
    from game_ai import get_rules_based_ai_move
    import random
    ```

2. **Creating the Main Window**

    Initialize Tkinter window: Set up the main window for the game.

    ```python
    root = tk.Tk()
    root.title('Tic-Tac-Toe')
    ```

3. **Setting Up the Game Board**

    Create buttons: Each cell in the Tic-Tac-Toe grid is a button. Define a function to create buttons and place them in a grid layout.

    ```python
    buttons = []
    board = initialize_board()

    def create_button(row, col):
        button = tk.Button(root, text='', width=10, height=3,
                           command=lambda: button_click(row, col))
        button.grid(row=row, column=col)
        return button
    ```

```
for row in range(3):
    button_row = []
    for col in range(3):
        button = create_button(row, col)
        button_row.append(button)
    buttons.append(button_row)
```

4. **Handling Button Clicks**

   Update game state: Define a function to handle button clicks, update the game state, and check for a winner or a draw.

   ```
   current_player = X_PLAYER
   computer_player = random.choice([X_PLAYER, O_PLAYER])
   status_label = tk.Label(root,
                           text=f"Player {current_player}'s Turn",
                           font=('Helvetica', 12))
   status_label.grid(row=3, columnspan=3)

   def button_click(row, col):
       global current_player
       if board[row * 3 + col] == ' ':
           board[row * 3 + col] = current_player
           buttons[row][col].config(text=current_player)

           if check_winner(board):
               messagebox.showinfo("Game Over", f"Player {current_player} wins!")
               reset_board()
           elif check_draw(board):
               messagebox.showinfo("Game Over", "The game is a draw!")
               reset_board()
           else:
               current_player = O_PLAYER if current_player == X_PLAYER else X_PLAYER
               status_label.config(text=f"Player {current_player}'s Turn")

               if current_player == computer_player:
                   ai_move()
   ```

5. **Implementing AI Moves**

   AI logic: Define a function for the AI to make a move.

   ```
   def ai_move():
       global current_player
       move = get_rules_based_ai_move(computer_player, board)
       board[move] = computer_player
       row, col = divmod(move, 3)
       buttons[row][col].config(text=computer_player)
   ```

```
        if check_winner(board):
            messagebox.showinfo("Game Over", f"Player {computer_player} wins!")
            reset_board()
        elif check_draw(board):
            messagebox.showinfo("Game Over", "The game is a draw!")
            reset_board()
        else:
            current_player = O_PLAYER if current_player == X_PLAYER else X_PLAYER
            status_label.config(text=f"Player {current_player}'s Turn")
```

6. **Resetting the Game**

   Reset board: Define a function to reset the game board.

```
def reset_board():
    global board, current_player
    board = initialize_board()
    current_player = X_PLAYER
    for row in range(3):
        for col in range(3):
            buttons[row][col].config(text='')
    status_label.config(text=f"Player {current_player}'s Turn")
```

7. **Running the Game**

   Start the Tkinter main loop: Ensure the main loop is started to run the GUI application.

```
if __name__ == "__main__":
    root.mainloop()
```

# Chapter 8: Exploring the Future: Where to Go from Here

Congratulations on reaching the end of our Python journey together! Well, it's more of a milestone. A significant one as well.

By now, you've laid a solid foundation in Python programming, and you're equipped with the skills to tackle a variety of projects. But where do you go from here? The answer is anywhere you want! Python is a remarkably versatile language used in fields as diverse as web development, data science, machine learning, automation, and even game development. The opportunities are endless, and your Python skills are the key to unlocking them.

The goal of this book has been to lay down a strong foundation for you in the world of computer programming, and Python in particular. This foundation is just the beginning.

**Words of Wisdom**: Remember the advice at the beginning of this book: everything we learn is built upon little by little, precept-upon-precept, concept-upon-concept. This approach is essential for developing unshakeable skills and confidence. Everyone must learn this way. There is a vast amount of knowledge out there for you to acquire. Be patient with yourself and others as you grow to acquire it. All knowledge, great or small, is achieved line-upon-line, precept-upon-precept, concept-upon-concept. Here a little, there a little. Until you have acquired much of it. But you still haven't scratched the surface. So, don't get a big head and go back to work.

# Chapter 8: Exploring the Future: Where to Go from Here

In this final chapter, we'll explore some of the most exciting and impactful areas where Python is used today. We'll also provide links and references to essential libraries and resources to help you continue your learning journey. Whether you're looking to build a career, start a hobby project, or simply learn more about what Python can do, this chapter will guide you on your next steps.

## 8.1 Fields Where Python is Used

Python's versatility and ease of use have made it a go-to language in many fields. As you continue your journey, consider exploring these areas where Python plays a pivotal role. Each field offers unique opportunities and challenges, allowing you to apply your Python skills in various exciting and impactful ways.

## 8.2 Web Development

Python can be used to create server-side web applications. With frameworks like Django and Flask, Python makes designing and maintaining secure, scalable, and maintainable web applications easy.

- **Django**: A high-level web framework that encourages rapid development and clean, pragmatic design. It includes many built-in features, such as authentication, an admin interface, and an ORM (Object-Relational Mapping) for database interactions.

    Django Documentation
    https://docs.djangoproject.com/

- **Flask**: A micro-framework that provides the essentials to get started with web development without imposing any constraints on how you should structure your application. It's lightweight and flexible, making it ideal for smaller projects or developers who want more control over their application's components.

    Flask Project
    https://flask.palletsprojects.com/

## 8.3 Data Science

Data scientists use Python for data analysis, visualization, and machine learning. Libraries like Pandas, NumPy, and Matplotlib simplify data manipulation and visualization, while Scikit-learn and TensorFlow provide tools for machine learning.

- **Pandas**: A powerful library for data manipulation and analysis. It provides data structures like DataFrames, which allow you to work with structured data easily and efficiently.

    Pandas Documentation
    https://pandas.pydata.org/pandas-docs/stable/

- **NumPy**: The fundamental package for numerical computing in Python. It provides support for arrays, matrices, and many mathematical functions to operate on these data structures.

    NumPy Documentation
    https://numpy.org/doc/

- **Scikit-learn**: A library for machine learning that provides simple and efficient tools for data mining and data analysis. It is built on NumPy, SciPy, and Matplotlib.

    Scikit-learn Documentation
    https://scikit-learn.org/stable/

- **TensorFlow**: An end-to-end open-source platform for machine learning. It has a comprehensive ecosystem of tools, libraries, and community resources.

    TensorFlow Documentation
    https://www.tensorflow.org/

## 8.4 Artificial Intelligence (AI)

Python is a primary language for AI due to its simplicity and the wide range of AI libraries and frameworks available, like Keras and PyTorch, which facilitate the development of neural networks and other AI models.

- **Keras**: A high-level neural networks API, written in Python and capable of running on top of TensorFlow, CNTK, or Theano. It allows for easy and fast prototyping.

    Keras Documentation
    https://keras.io/

- **PyTorch**: An open-source machine learning library based on the Torch library. It provides a flexible and dynamic interface for building neural networks.

   PyTorch Documentation
  https://pytorch.org

## 8.5 Scientific Computing

Python is widely used in scientific research for its ability to handle and process large datasets, perform complex calculations, and simulate systems. SciPy and NumPy are two key libraries in this field.

- **SciPy**: A Python library used for scientific and technical computing. It builds on NumPy and provides a large number of functions that operate on NumPy arrays.

   SciPy Documentation
  https://docs.scipy.org/doc/scipy/reference/

## 8.6 Automation and Scripting

Python's simplicity makes it a popular choice for writing scripts to automate repetitive tasks and processes on computers without the need to develop complete programs.

- **Selenium**: A tool for automating web browsers. You can use it to perform automated testing of web applications or to scrape data from websites.

   Selenium Documentation
  https://www.selenium.dev/documentation

- **BeautifulSoup**: A library for parsing HTML and XML documents. It provides Pythonic idioms for iterating, searching, and modifying the parse tree, which makes it easy to scrape information from web pages.

   BeautifulSoup Documentation
  https://www.crummy.com/software/BeautifulSoup/bs4/doc/

## 8.7 Software Development

Python is often used for developing desktop and command-line applications. It's valued for rapid development and cross-platform compatibility with tools like PyQt and Tkinter.

- **PyQt** is a set of Python bindings for Qt libraries that can be used to create cross-platform applications with a native look and feel.

    PyQt Documentation
    https://www.riverbankcomputing.com/software/pyqt/intro

- **Tkinter**: The standard GUI library for Python. Python when combined with Tkinter provides a fast and easy way to create GUI applications.

    Tkinter Documentation
    https://docs.python.org/3/library/tkinter.html

## 8.8 Game Development

Python's Pygame library is a set of Python modules designed for writing video games. It includes graphics and sound libraries, making it suitable for game prototyping and development.

- **Pygame**: A set of Python modules designed for writing video games. It includes computer graphics and sound libraries.

    Pygame Documentation
    https://www.pygame.org/docs/

## 8.9 Network Programming

Python provides libraries like socket which is used in network programming for tasks such as writing servers and client applications, network sniffing, and protocol analysis.

- **socket**: A low-level networking interface in Python that provides access to the BSD socket interface. It allows you to create network connections and transfer data between servers and clients.

    Socket Documentation
    https://docs.python.org/3/library/socket.html

CHAPTER 8: EXPLORING THE FUTURE: WHERE TO GO FROM HERE

## 8.10 Finance

Python is extensively used in quantitative finance to analyze financial markets, back-test trading strategies, calculate financial risk, and build algorithmic trading systems with libraries like QuantLib and Pyalgotrade.

- **QuantLib**: A library for quantitative finance that provides tools for pricing derivatives, managing portfolios, and more.

    QuantLib Documentation
    https://www.quantlib.org/

- **Pyalgotrade**: A Python library for backtesting trading strategies.

    Pyalgotrade Documentation
    https://github.com/gbeced/pyalgotrade

## 8.11 Chapter Summary

As you can see, Python's versatility knows no bounds. Its simplicity and readability have made it the go-to choice for beginners and seasoned developers. Python's wide-ranging applications indicate that each area it touches offers enough depth for entire books on just that subject alone. This book is designed to give you a solid start with Python, equipping you with the basics. As you become more comfortable with the language, you'll find that you can dive deeper into any specific area that interests you. Think of this as the first step on your journey—you'll have plenty of opportunities to specialize and explore topics in detail as you gain more experience and confidence.

# Share Your Passion for Python!

Now that you've completed this Python journey, you're in the perfect position to share your thoughts with others. By leaving a short review, you can help more people discover Python and unlock their own possibilities.

Your honest opinion will not only help new readers kickstart their own Python journey but will also help me create even more helpful guides for aspiring programmers.

**Thank you for taking the time to share your feedback—it means the world!**

*Scan the QR code below…*

Amazon
Absolute Beginner's Guide to Python Programming
https://www.amazon.com/review/create-review/?asin=1964520002

# Conclusion

As you reach the end of this book, it's essential to reflect on the journey we've taken together. From the initial steps of setting up Python to exploring its wide-ranging applications, you've built a solid foundation in programming. Python's versatility knows no bounds. Its simplicity and readability have made it the go-to choice for beginners and seasoned developers.

## Embrace the Endless Possibilities

Python's wide-ranging applications indicate that each area it touches offers enough depth for entire books on just that subject alone. This book is designed to give you a solid start with Python, equipping you with the basics. As you become more comfortable with the language, you'll find that you can dive deeper into any specific area that interests you. Think of this as the first step on your journey—you'll have plenty of opportunities to specialize and explore topics in detail as you gain more experience and confidence.

## The Art of Falling

Don't be afraid of making mistakes. Every error is an opportunity to learn and grow. As you continue to explore Python, you will encounter challenges. Embrace them. Falling and getting back up is how you build resilience and expertise. Remember, the path to mastery is not a straight line but a journey filled with twists and turns.

## Building a Strong Foundation

You've developed a solid understanding of Python's basics. This knowledge is your toolkit. As you continue to build upon this foundation, you will find that the skills you've gained here will support you in tackling more advanced topics and projects. Whether it's web development, data science, machine learning, or any other field, the fundamentals you've learned will always be your guide.

## The Balance of Learning

The world of programming is vast and can seem overwhelming. But remember, learning is a journey. Each new concept and project builds upon what you already know. By continuously adding to your knowledge, you expand your capabilities and confidence. Take each step with patience and curiosity, and you'll find joy in the process of discovery.

## Encouragement for the Future

The chapters of this book have guided you through some of the most exciting areas where Python is used today. You've found links and references to essential libraries and resources to help you continue your learning journey. Whether you're looking to build a career, start a hobby project, or simply learn more about what Python can do, this book has aimed to provide you with a roadmap for your next steps.

## Final Thoughts

Python is not just a tool but a gateway to endless possibilities. As you progress, keep experimenting, learning, and, most importantly, enjoy the journey. Your path to mastery has just begun, and the world of Python is at your fingertips. Dive in, explore, and let your creativity soar.

Thank you for embarking on this journey with me. I wish you all the best in your Python programming endeavors.

# APPENDIX A: EXERCISE SOLUTIONS

**A Note on Using These Solutions:** It is not cheating to peek at the solutions to the exercises or chapter projects (available on GitHub). However, I recommend you put your best effort into solving the problems independently before looking at the solutions provided. These exercises and projects aim to help you learn and understand the concepts covered in each chapter.

Remember, everyone's learning process is unique. Struggling with and working through a problem can be valuable to learning. So, take your time; feel free to consult my solutions when you are stuck. You know yourself best, and you'll know when it's the right time to check out the provided solutions.

## Chapter 2 Solutions

### Exercise 1: Basic Variable Assignment

```python
# Assigning values to variables
my_integer = 10
my_float = 20.5
my_string = "Hello, Python!"
my_boolean = True

# Printing the values
print("Integer:", my_integer)
print("Float:", my_float)
print("String:", my_string)
print("Boolean:", my_boolean)
```

### Exercise 2: Type Conversion

```python
# Taking user input and converting to integer
user_input = input("Enter a number: ")
user_number = int(user_input)
result = user_number * 2
print("Double your number is:", result)
```

### Exercise 3: String Formatting

```python
# Using f-string
name = "Alice"
age = 30
print(f"Hello, {name}. You are {age} years old.")

# Using format() method
temperature = 23.45678
print("The current temperature is {:.2f}°C.".format(temperature))
```

# Appendix A: Exercise Solutions

## Exercise 4: Control Structures

```python
# Checking if a number is positive, negative, or zero
number = int(input("Enter a number: "))
if number > 0:
    print("The number is positive.")
elif number < 0:
    print("The number is negative.")
else:
    print("The number is zero.")
```

## Exercise 5: Arithmetic Operations

```python
# Performing arithmetic operations
num1 = float(input("Enter the first number: "))
num2 = float(input("Enter the second number: "))

print("Addition:", num1 + num2)
print("Subtraction:", num1 - num2)
print("Multiplication:", num1 * num2)
print("Division:", num1 / num2)
print("Exponentiation:", num1 ** num2)
```

## Exercise 6: Comparison and Logical Operators

```python
# Determining age category
age = int(input("Enter your age: "))
if age < 13:
    print("You are a child.")
elif age >= 13 and age < 18:
    print("You are a teenager.")
elif age >= 18 and age < 65:
    print("You are an adult.")
else:
    print("You are a senior.")
```

## Exercise 7: Ternary Conditional Expression

```python
# Checking if a number is even or odd
number = int(input("Enter a number: "))
result = "even" if number % 2 == 0 else "odd"
print(f"The number is {result}.")
```

# Chapter 3 Solutions

## Exercise 1: List Manipulation

```python
# Create a list of your favorite movies
favorite_movies = ["Inception", "The Matrix", "Interstellar"]

# Add two more movies
```

```python
favorite_movies.append("The Godfather")
favorite_movies.append("Pulp Fiction")

# Remove one movie
favorite_movies.remove("The Matrix")

# Print the updated list
print(favorite_movies)  # Output: ['Inception', 'Interstellar', 'The Godfather', 'Pulp Fiction']
```

## Exercise 2: 2D Array Access

```python
# Create a 3x3 matrix
matrix = [
    [1, 2, 3],
    [4, 5, 6],
    [7, 8, 9]
]

# Print each element using nested loops
for row in matrix:
    for element in row:
        print(element)
```

## Exercise 3: Dictionary Operations

```python
# Create a dictionary with information about a book
book_info = {
    "title": "1984",
    "author": "George Orwell",
    "year": 1949
}

# Add a key for genre and update the year
book_info["genre"] = "Dystopian"
book_info["year"] = 1950

# Print all keys and values
for key, value in book_info.items():
    print(f"{key}: {value}")
```

## Exercise 4: Set Operations

```python
# Create a set of unique words from a given sentence
sentence = "the quick brown fox jumps over the lazy dog"
words = sentence.split()
unique_words = set(words)

# Print the set of unique words
print(unique_words)
```

Appendix A: Exercise Solutions

## Exercise 5: For Loop Practice

```python
# Write a for loop to print the first 10 numbers in the Fibonacci sequence
a, b = 0, 1
for _ in range(10):
    print(a)
    a, b = b, a + b
```

## Exercise 6: While Loop Practice

```python
# Write a while loop to reverse a string
original_string = "hello"
reversed_string = ""
index = len(original_string) - 1

while index >= 0:
    reversed_string += original_string[index]
    index -= 1

print(reversed_string)  # Output: 'olleh'
```

## Exercise 7: Combined Data Types

```python
# Create a list of dictionaries, each representing a student with name and grade
students = [
    {"name": "Alice", "grade": 90},
    {"name": "Bob", "grade": 85},
    {"name": "Charlie", "grade": 95}
]

# Print each student's name and grade using a loop
for student in students:
    print(f"Name: {student['name']}, Grade: {student['grade']}")
```

# Chapter 4 Solutions

## Exercise 1: Basic Function Creation

```python
def sum_numbers(numbers):
    return sum(numbers)
```

## Exercise 2: Scope and Lifetime

```python
total = 0

def modify_global():
    global total
    total += 10

def use_local():
```

```
    total = 5
    print("Local total:", total)
```

## Exercise 3: Using Standard Modules

```
import math

def circle_area(radius):
    return math.pi * (radius ** 2)
```

## Exercise 4: Creating and Importing Custom Modules

```
# mymodule.py
def is_prime(n):
    if n <= 1:
        return False
    for i in range(2, int(n ** 0.5) + 1):
        if n % i == 0:
            return False
    return True

# main.py
from mymodule import is_prime

print(is_prime(11))  # True
```

## Exercise 5: Working with Packages

```
mypackage/
├── __init__.py
├── module1.py
└── module2.py

# module1.py
def greet(name):
    return f"Hello, {name}!"

# module2.py
def farewell(name):
    return f"Goodbye, {name}!"

# main.py
from mypackage.module1 import greet
from mypackage.module2 import farewell

print(greet("Alice"))    # Hello, Alice!
print(farewell("Alice")) # Goodbye, Alice!
```

# Appendix A: Exercise Solutions

## Exercise 6: Lambda Functions

```python
data = [(1, 'b'), (3, 'a'), (2, 'c')]
sorted_data = sorted(data, key=lambda x: x[1])
print(sorted_data)  # [(3, 'a'), (1, 'b'), (2, 'c')]
```

# Chapter 5 Solutions

## Exercise 1: Reading from a Text File

```python
def read_file(file_path):
    try:
        with open(file_path, 'r') as file:
            content = file.read()
            print(content)
    except FileNotFoundError:
        print("The file was not found.")
    except PermissionError:
        print("You do not have permission to read this file.")
    except Exception as e:
        print(f"An unexpected error occurred: {e}")

read_file('journal.txt')
```

## Exercise 2: Writing to a Text File

```python
def write_to_file(file_path, content):
    try:
        with open(file_path, 'w') as file:
            file.write(content)
    except Exception as e:
        print(f"An error occurred: {e}")

write_to_file('journal.txt', '2024-05-25: Learned about file handling in Python.\n')
```

## Exercise 3: Appending to a Text File

```python
def append_to_file(file_path, content):
    try:
        with open(file_path, 'a') as file:
            file.write(content)
    except Exception as e:
        print(f"An error occurred: {e}")

append_to_file('journal.txt', '2024-05-26: Practiced writing and reading files.\n')
```

## Exercise 4: Reading from a JSON File

```python
import json

def read_json(file_path):
```

```
    try:
        with open(file_path, 'r') as file:
            data = json.load(file)
            print(data)
    except FileNotFoundError:
        print("The file was not found.")
    except json.JSONDecodeError:
        print("Error decoding JSON.")
    except Exception as e:
        print(f"An unexpected error occurred: {e}")

read_json('expenses.json')
```

## Exercise 5: Writing to a JSON File

```
import json

expenses = [
    {"date": "2024-05-25", "amount": 50.75, "category": "Grocery", "description": "Weekly groceries"},
    {"date": "2024-05-26", "amount": 120.00, "category": "Utilities", "description": "Electricity bill"}
]

def write_json(file_path, data):
    try:
        with open(file_path, 'w') as file:
            json.dump(data, file, indent=4)
    except Exception as e:
        print(f"An error occurred: {e}")

write_json('expenses.json', expenses)
```

## Exercise 6: Adding a New Expense to a JSON File

```
import json

def add_expense(file_path, new_expense):
    try:
        with open(file_path, 'r') as file:
            expenses = json.load(file)
    except FileNotFoundError:
        expenses = []
    except json.JSONDecodeError:
        print("Error decoding JSON.")
        expenses = []
    except Exception as e:
        print(f"An unexpected error occurred: {e}")
        return

    expenses.append(new_expense)

    try:
```

# APPENDIX A: EXERCISE SOLUTIONS

```python
        with open(file_path, 'w') as file:
            json.dump(expenses, file, indent=4)
    except Exception as e:
        print(f"An error occurred: {e}")

new_expense = {"date": "2024-05-27", "amount": 75.20, "category": "Entertainment", "description":
"Concert tickets"}
add_expense('expenses.json', new_expense)
```

## Chapter 6 Solutions

### Exercise 1: Define and Use a Class

```python
class Book:
    def __init__(self, title, author, year):
        self.title = title
        self.author = author
        self.year = year

    def display_details(self):
        print(f"Title: {self.title}, Author: {self.author}, Year: {self.year}")

# Creating instances
book1 = Book("1984", "George Orwell", 1949)
book2 = Book("To Kill a Mockingbird", "Harper Lee", 1960)

# Displaying details
book1.display_details()
book2.display_details()
```

### Exercise 2: Use Composition

```python
class Library:
    def __init__(self):
        self.books = []

    def add_book(self, book):
        self.books.append(book)

    def display_books(self):
        for book in self.books:
            book.display_details()

# Creating instances of Book
book1 = Book("1984", "George Orwell", 1949)
book2 = Book("To Kill a Mockingbird", "Harper Lee", 1960)

# Creating an instance of Library and adding books
library = Library()
library.add_book(book1)
```

```
library.add_book(book2)

# Displaying all books in the library
library.display_books()
```

## Exercise 3: Implement Inheritance

```
class EBook(Book):
    def __init__(self, title, author, year, file_size):
        super().__init__(title, author, year)
        self.file_size = file_size

    def display_details(self):
        print(f"Title: {self.title}, Author: {self.author}, Year: {self.year}, File Size: {self.file_size}MB")

# Creating instances of EBook
ebook1 = EBook("1984", "George Orwell", 1949, 2)
ebook2 = EBook("To Kill a Mockingbird", "Harper Lee", 1960, 1.5)

# Displaying details
ebook1.display_details()
ebook2.display_details()
```

## Exercise 4: Demonstrate Polymorphism

```
def display_book_details(book):
    book.display_details()

# Creating instances of Book and EBook
book1 = Book("1984", "George Orwell", 1949)
ebook1 = EBook("1984", "George Orwell", 1949, 2)

# Demonstrating polymorphism
display_book_details(book1)
display_book_details(ebook1)
```

## Exercise 5: Use Abstraction

```
from abc import ABC, abstractmethod
import math

class Shape(ABC):
    @abstractmethod
    def calculate_area(self):
        pass

    @abstractmethod
```

```
        def calculate_perimeter(self):
            pass

class Circle(Shape):
    def __init__(self, radius):
        self.radius = radius

    def calculate_area(self):
        return math.pi * self.radius ** 2

    def calculate_perimeter(self):
        return 2 * math.pi * self.radius

class Rectangle(Shape):
    def __init__(self, length, width):
        self.length = length
        self.width = width

    def calculate_area(self):
        return self.length * self.width

    def calculate_perimeter(self):
        return 2 * (self.length + self.width)

# Creating instances and calling methods
circle = Circle(5)
rectangle = Rectangle(4, 7)

print(f"Circle Area: {circle.calculate_area()}, Perimeter: {circle.calculate_perimeter()}")
print(f"Rectangle Area: {rectangle.calculate_area()}, Perimeter: {rectangle.calculate_perimeter()}")
```

## Chapter 7 Solutions

### Exercise 1: Create a Simple Calculator

```
import tkinter as tk

def evaluate_expression(expression):
    try:
        result = eval(expression)
        return result
    except Exception as e:
        return "Error"

def on_button_click(char):
    if char == "=":
        result = evaluate_expression(entry.get())
        entry.delete(0, tk.END)
        entry.insert(tk.END, str(result))
    elif char == "C":
        entry.delete(0, tk.END)
    else:
```

```python
        entry.insert(tk.END, char)

root = tk.Tk()
root.title("Simple Calculator")

entry = tk.Entry(root, width=16, font=('Arial', 24), borderwidth=2, relief="solid")
entry.grid(row=0, column=0, columnspan=4)

buttons = [
    '7', '8', '9', '/',
    '4', '5', '6', '*',
    '1', '2', '3', '-',
    '0', 'C', '=', '+'
]

row_val = 1
col_val = 0

for button in buttons:
    action = lambda x=button: on_button_click(x)
    tk.Button(root, text=button, width=10, height=2, command=action).grid(row=row_val, column=col_val)
    col_val += 1
    if col_val > 3:
        col_val = 0
        row_val += 1

root.mainloop()
```

## Exercise 2: To-Do List Application

```python
import tkinter as tk
from tkinter import messagebox

def add_task():
    task = entry.get()
    if task != "":
        tasks_listbox.insert(tk.END, task)
        entry.delete(0, tk.END)
    else:
        messagebox.showwarning("Warning", "You must enter a task.")

def delete_task():
    try:
        task_index = tasks_listbox.curselection()[0]
        tasks_listbox.delete(task_index)
    except:
        messagebox.showwarning("Warning", "You must select a task to delete.")

root = tk.Tk()
root.title("To-Do List")

frame = tk.Frame(root)
```

```python
frame.pack(pady=10)

tasks_listbox = tk.Listbox(frame, width=50, height=10, bd=0)
tasks_listbox.pack(side=tk.LEFT, fill=tk.BOTH)

scrollbar = tk.Scrollbar(frame)
scrollbar.pack(side=tk.RIGHT, fill=tk.BOTH)

tasks_listbox.config(yscrollcommand=scrollbar.set)
scrollbar.config(command=tasks_listbox.yview)

entry = tk.Entry(root, width=50)
entry.pack(pady=10)

add_button = tk.Button(root, text="Add Task", command=add_task)
add_button.pack(pady=5)

delete_button = tk.Button(root, text="Delete Task", command=delete_task)
delete_button.pack(pady=5)

root.mainloop()
```

# APPENDIX B: GITHUB PRIMER FOR DOWNLOADING SOURCE CODE

GitHub is a web-based platform used for version control and collaboration. It allows multiple people to work on projects at the same time. While GitHub hosts a vast array of projects and supports numerous advanced features, this primer focuses on how you can download source code from a repository (repo) without needing a GitHub account. A repository is like a project's folder that contains all of its files, including documentation, and stores each file's revision history.

## Accessing and Downloading Code from GitHub

### Step 1: Finding the Repository

- Throughout this book, you'll encounter links or QR codes directing you to specific GitHub repositories. Click on the link or scan the QR code with your smartphone to navigate to the GitHub page where the source code is hosted.

### Step 2: Navigating the Repository

- Once you're on the repository page, you'll see a list of files and folders associated with the project. You might also see a description and additional information, such as recent updates, above the file list.

### Step 3: Downloading the Source Code

- To download the entire repository:
  - Look for a green button labeled **Code** near the top of the page. Click on it to open a dropdown menu.
  - In the dropdown menu, find and click the **Download ZIP** option. This action will download the repository as a ZIP file to your computer.
  - Locate the ZIP file in your Downloads folder (or wherever you've set your browser to save downloads), and extract it using your operating system's file extraction utility. After extraction, you'll have access to all the files contained in the repository.

## Tips for Using Downloaded Code

- **Exploring the Repository**: Once you've extracted the files, take some time to explore the folder structure. Repositories often include a `README.md` file, which contains important information about the project, including how to set it up and use it.

APPENDIX B: GITHUB PRIMER FOR DOWNLOADING SOURCE CODE

- **Requirements**: Some projects may require additional setup, such as installing dependencies. This information is typically found in the `README.md` file or a separate `INSTALLATION.md` file.
- **Seeking Help**: If you encounter any issues, check the repository's `ISSUES` tab for solutions or to ask questions. Though you'll need a GitHub account to post issues, browsing existing issues can be done without an account.

## No GitHub Account Required

As outlined, downloading files from GitHub does not require a GitHub account. This makes it easy for anyone to access and use the source code for projects, even without being a part of the GitHub community.

We encourage you to explore the repositories linked throughout this book. Each repository offers a unique opportunity to learn from real-world code examples and apply what you've learned in a practical context.

# APPENDIX C: SELF-DOCUMENTING CODE: WRITING CODE THAT EXPLAINS ITSELF

In the journey of mastering Python, you'll come across a powerful concept that elevates the clarity and maintainability of your code: self-documenting code. This approach is about crafting your code in such a way that anyone reading it can easily understand its purpose and operation without the need for extensive external comments or documentation.

The essence of self-documenting code lies in the choice of meaningful variable and function names, the code's structure, and its logic's simplicity. By adhering to clear naming conventions and organizing your code logically, you make it intuitive for others (and your future self) to grasp what the code does, why it does it, and how it does it.

## Key Characteristics of Self-Documenting Code

1. **Descriptive Names**: Choose variable, function, and class names that reflect their purpose and the type of data they handle. For example, `calculate_total_income` is more informative than just `calculate`.
2. **Simplicity**: Keep the code simple and straightforward. Complex logic is harder to understand and maintain, even with good naming conventions.
3. **Consistency**: Use consistent naming conventions and coding styles throughout your project. This will help readers quickly become familiar with your code's patterns.
4. **Minimal Comments**: While comments are essential for explaining the "why" behind certain decisions, overly commenting can clutter the code. Well-written code minimizes the need for comments by being clear and concise in its actions.
5. **Function and Variable Scope**: Keep functions focused on a single task and variables scoped as narrowly as possible. This clarity of responsibility aids in understanding the code's functionality.
6. **Code Formatting**: For code formatting, adhere to Python's style guide (PEP 8). Well-formatted code is easier to read and understand.
7. **Avoid Magic Numbers**: Replace numbers with named constants to explain their meaning. For instance, use `MAX_RETRY_LIMIT = 5` instead of a lone number 5, which leaves readers guessing its significance.

## Benefits of Self-Documenting Code

- **Improved Readability**: Makes the code more readable and understandable without relying on external documentation.
- **Ease of Maintenance**: Simplifies debugging and modifying the code, as its purpose and mechanism are clear.

- **Better Collaboration**: Facilitates smoother collaboration among team members, as the code's intent is easily grasped by everyone.

Self-documenting code is not about eliminating comments or documentation but about reducing the reliance on them by writing code that is as clear and understandable as possible. It's a practice that, when mastered, significantly enhances the quality and longevity of your software projects.

# Appendix D: Choosing the Right IDE

In the Python world, there are excellent IDE options to consider, and lots of them cater to a range of expertise from beginners to seasoned developers. The 2023 Stack Overflow survey offers insights into IDE popularity and user satisfaction, guiding our curated list of 8 popular Python IDEs. Each IDE is unique, with specific features, benefits, and suited project types, ensuring there's an ideal environment for every programmer's needs.

Stack Overflow
Integrated Development Environment
https://survey.stackoverflow.co/2023/#section-most-popular-technologies-integrated-development-environment

We provide a convenient way to explore these IDEs further through anchor URLs and QR codes for each, accommodating both digital and print readers. As you evaluate these options, consider the IDE's features in relation to your coding style, project requirements, and the value of its community and support. The goal is to find an IDE that enhances your efficiency and enjoyment of Python programming, making your coding journey as intuitive and productive as possible.

Here is a brief list of the more popular IDEs:

## Visual Studio Code (VS Code)

Visual Studio Code is one of the most popular choices among developers. It's renowned for its user-friendly interface, extensive library of extensions, and robust debugging capabilities. Plus, it's completely free to use, making it an ideal choice for both beginners and professionals. VS Code is a generic IDE. As a result, it needs further configuration to work with Python.

Microsoft
Visual Studio Code Download
https://code.visualstudio.com/download

## PyCharm

PyCharm is a powerful and widely used IDE specifically designed for Python. It offers features like code analysis, intelligent code completion, and a variety of tools for web development, scientific computing, and data science. If you like JetBrains other IDEs, like IntelliJ (Java), this is an excellent option. PyCharm was specifically written for Python. As a result, it doesn't require much more configuration to start using it. There are two versions: Community Edition

# APPENDIX D: CHOOSING THE RIGHT IDE

(which is free) and Pro Edition (not so much). Check out this website to compare the editions and download:

---

JetBrains
PyCharm Community and Professional Editions Explained
https://blog.jetbrains.com/pycharm/2017/09/pycharm-community-edition-and-professional-edition-explained-licenses-and-more/

---

## Jupyter Notebook

Jupyter Notebook is an interactive computing environment that's excellent for data analysis and scientific computing. It allows you to write and execute Python code in a document-style format, making it great for experimentation and documentation. Jupyter Notebook supports 40+ languages. It will require further configuration to work with Python.

---

Jupyter Network
https://jupyter.org/

---

## Spyder

Spyder is an IDE tailored for scientific and data-driven Python development. It provides a MATLAB-like interface with features like variable exploration, data visualization, and integrated IPython support. https://www.spyder-ide.org/

---

Spyder
The Scientific Python Development Environment
https://www.spyder-ide.org/

---

## Thonny

Thonny is a beginner-friendly IDE designed to simplify Python programming for learners. It has a straightforward interface and includes features like code completion, debugger, and a built-in package manager.

---

Thonny
Python IDE for Beginners
https://thonny.org/

---

## IDLE (Python's Built-in IDE)

Python comes with its own basic IDE called IDLE. It's a simple and lightweight option for beginners to get started quickly. While it lacks some advanced features, it's a good choice for basic Python scripting. Since IDLE comes with Python and well…you will be installing Python in the next section, here is a link to its documentation:

Python.org
IDLE is Python's Integrated Development and Learning Environment
https://docs.python.org/3/library/idle.html

## PyDev (for Eclipse)

If you're already using the Eclipse IDE, you can add the PyDev plugin to enable Python development within Eclipse. It offers features like code analysis, debugging, and an integrated Python console.

PyDev
Eclipse AddOn
https://www.pydev.org/download.html

## Anaconda Navigator

Anaconda Navigator is a platform that includes a variety of data science and machine learning tools. It provides a user-friendly interface for managing Python packages and environments and includes the Jupyter Notebook IDE.

Anaconda Distribution
Free Download
https://www.anaconda.com/download/

As far as this book is concerned, choosing an integrated development environment (IDE) is entirely up to you, and it is tailored to meet your needs as a learner and developer.

We understand that each programmer's journey is unique, with diverse preferences, project requirements, and learning styles. Therefore, we encourage you to select an IDE that aligns with your personal goals, enhances your coding experience, and supports your growth in Python programming. Whether you prioritize a rich set of features, an intuitive user interface, or robust community support, the most important factor is finding an environment where you feel comfortable and empowered to explore the vast possibilities of Python.

# GLOSSARY

**Abstract Base Class:** A module in Python that provides the infrastructure for defining abstract classes and methods. (ch. 6)

**Abstract Class:** A class that cannot be instantiated on its own and is designed to be subclassed. Abstract classes typically contain one or more abstract methods. (ch. 6)

**Abstract Method:** A method that is declared in an abstract class but does not have an implementation. Subclasses of the abstract class are required to provide an implementation for the abstract method. (ch. 6)

**API:** Application Programmers Interface. A set of rules and protocols that allow different software applications to communicate and interact with each other. (ch. 7)

**Arithmetic Operators:** Symbols that represent basic mathematical operations, such as +, -, *, /, and **. (ch. 2)

**BASH:** See Command Prompt (ch. 1)

**BeautifulSoup:** A library for parsing HTML and XML documents, providing Pythonic idioms for iterating, searching, and modifying the parse tree, making it easy to scrape information from web pages. (ch. 8)

**Boolean:** A data type that can hold one of two values: True or False. Example: is_python_fun = True (ch. 1)

**break Statement:** Exits a loop. (ch. 3)

**Button:** A Button is a widget in Tkinter that users can click to trigger actions. It is crucial for creating interactive applications. (ch. 7)

**Callback Function:** A Callback Function in Tkinter is a function that is called when a specific event occurs, such as a button click. (ch. 7)

**Child Class:** See Subclass (ch. 6)

**Class:** A blueprint or template for creating objects. It defines a set of attributes (properties) and methods (behaviors) that the objects created from the class will have. (ch. 6)

**Command Prompt:** A text-based interface used to run commands on the operating system. Example: Command Prompt on Windows, Terminal on macOS and Linux. (ch. 1)

**Comparison Operators:** Symbols that compare two values, returning a boolean result, such as ==, !=, >, =, and <=. (ch. 2)

**Compiler:** A tool that translates a program written in a high-level language into machine code, which the computer's processor can execute directly. (ch. 1)

**Composition:** A principle where objects are constructed using other objects, allowing for complex structures by combining simpler ones. It involves including instances of other classes as attributes within a class. (ch. 6)

**Concatenation:** The operation of joining two strings together using the + operator. Example: "Hello, " + "World!" results in "Hello, World!" (ch. 1)

**continue Statement:** Skips the current iteration of a loop. (ch. 3)

**Control Structure:** A block of programming that determines the flow of control based on specified conditions, including if, elif, else statements. (ch. 2)

# Glossary

**CRUD:** An acronym for Create, Read, Update, and Delete, representing the basic operations performed on data in a database or a similar system. (ch. 7)

**CSV File:** Comma-Separated Values. A simple text format for storing tabular data where each line represents a data record, and each record consists of fields separated by commas. (ch. 5)

**Data Science:** An interdisciplinary field that uses scientific methods, algorithms, and systems to extract knowledge and insights from structured and unstructured data. It involves data collection, cleaning, analysis, and visualization to inform decision-making.

**Data Type:** A classification that specifies which type of value a variable can hold in programming, such as integer, float, string, or boolean. (ch. 2)

**Default Button:** The Default Button in a Tkinter message box is the button that is pre-selected when the message box appears, which can be activated by pressing the Enter key. (ch. 7)

**Dictionary:** A collection of key-value pairs. (ch. 3)

**Django:** A high-level web framework that encourages rapid development and clean, pragmatic design, including built-in features such as authentication, an admin interface, and an ORM for database interactions. (ch. 8)

**Duck Typing:** A concept in dynamically typed languages like Python where an object's type is determined by its behavior (methods and properties) rather than its explicit class. It follows "If it looks like a duck and quacks like a duck, it must be a duck." (ch. 6)

**Dynamic Typing:** A feature of Python where the type of a variable is interpreted at runtime, meaning you don't have to declare the type of a variable explicitly. (ch. 1)

**Encapsulation:** The concept of bundling data and methods that operate on that data within a single unit or class. Encapsulation also involves hiding the internal state and requiring all interaction to be performed through an object's methods. (ch. 6)

**Entry:** An Entry is a widget in Tkinter that allows users to input a single line of text. It is commonly used in forms and data input scenarios. (ch. 7)

**Environment Variable:** A variable outside of the Python program that can affect the behavior of running processes. Often used to set paths and other system-wide settings. Example: PATH in the operating system's environment. (ch. 1)

**Event Loop:** The Event Loop is a loop in GUI programming that waits for and dispatches events or messages in a program. In Tkinter, root.mainloop() starts the event loop, allowing the application to respond to user actions. (ch. 7)

**except Statement:** See try/except/finally

**File Handling:** The process of opening, reading, writing, and closing files in a programming language. (ch. 5)

**filter Function:** Constructs a list from those elements of the input list for which a function returns true. (ch. 4)

**finally Statement:** See try/except/finally

**Flask:** A micro-framework that provides the essentials to get started with web development without imposing constraints on application structure, making it ideal for smaller projects or developers wanting more control. (ch. 8)

**Float:** A data type representing numbers with a fractional component, denoted by a decimal point. Example: 3.14, 0.923 (ch. 1)

**For Loop:** Iterates over a sequence. (ch. 3)

**format() Method:** A method for formatting strings in Python, which allows insertion of variables and expressions into strings using curly braces {} as placeholders. (ch. 2)

**Frame:** A Frame is a container widget in Tkinter that can hold and organize other widgets. It is useful for complex layouts and grouping related elements together. (ch. 7)

**F-String:** A formatted string literal in Python, introduced in Python 3.6, that allows expressions to be embedded inside string literals, using curly braces {}. (ch. 2)

**Function:** A block of organized, reusable code that performs a single action. Functions can take inputs (arguments) and return an output (result). Example: def greet(name): return "Hello " + name (ch. 1)

**Global Variable:** A variable that is accessible from anywhere in the code. (ch. 4)

**Grid:** The grid() method in Tkinter places widgets into a grid of rows and columns, providing more complex layouts. (ch. 7)

**GUI:** Graphical User Interface (GUI) is a type of user interface that allows users to interact with electronic devices through graphical icons and visual indicators, as opposed to text-based interfaces. (ch. 7)

**IDE (Integrated Development Environment):** A software application that provides comprehensive facilities to computer programmers for software development. An IDE typically includes a code editor, a debugger, and build automation tools. Example: PyCharm, Visual Studio Code, Jupyter Notebook (ch. 1)

**Immutability:** A property of data types where the value cannot be changed after it is created, such as with strings and tuples. (ch. 2)

**Indentation:** The use of whitespace (spaces or tabs) at the beginning of lines to define the level of nesting and structure in Python code. (ch. 2)

**Inheritance:** A mechanism in which one class (subclass or child class) inherits attributes and methods from another class (superclass or parent class). It allows for code reuse and the creation of a hierarchical relationship between classes. (ch. 6)

**INI File:** A simple text file with a basic structure composed of sections, properties, and values, commonly used for configuration settings. (ch. 5)

**Input Function:** A built-in Python function that allows the program to receive input from the user. Example: user_name = input("What is your name? ") (ch. 1)

**Integer:** A data type representing whole numbers without a fractional component. Example: 10, -3 (ch. 1)

**Interpreter:** A program that reads and executes code written in a programming language. The Python interpreter reads and executes Python code line by line. (ch. 1)

**JSON:** JavaScript Object Notation. A lightweight data-interchange format that is easy for humans to read and write and easy for machines to parse and generate. (ch. 5)

#Deleted

**Label:** A Label is a widget in Tkinter used to display text or images. It is often used to provide information to the user. (ch. 7)

**Lambda Function:** An anonymous function defined using the lambda keyword. (ch. 4)

**Layout Manager:** Layout Managers in Tkinter (such as pack(), grid(), and place()) are used to control the positioning and sizing of widgets within a window. (ch. 7)

**List:** An ordered collection of items. (ch. 3)

**Local Variable:** A variable that is only accessible within the function or block where it is defined. (ch. 4)

**Logical Operators:** Operators that combine multiple boolean expressions or values, including and, or, and not. (ch. 2)

**Loop:** A control structure that repeatedly executes a block of code. (ch. 3)

**map Function:** Applies a given function to all items in an input list. (ch. 4)

**Message Box:** A Message Box is a popup dialog in Tkinter used to display messages to the user. It can be informational, warning, or error messages, and can also ask for user confirmation. (ch. 7)

**Method Overloading:** A feature in OOP where a subclass provides a specific implementation of a method that is already defined in its superclass. The overridden method in the subclass has the same name and parameters as the method in the superclass. (ch. 6)

**Module:** A file containing Python definitions and statements. (ch. 4)

**Nested Loop:** A loop inside another loop. (ch. 3)

**NumPy:** The fundamental package for numerical computing in Python, supporting arrays, matrices, and many mathematical functions to operate on these data structures. (ch. 8)

**Object:** An instance of a class that encapsulates data and functionality. Objects are the actual entities that are manipulated in OOP. (ch. 6)

**OOP:** Object Oriented Programming. A programming paradigm that uses objects and classes to structure software in a way that models real-world entities and their interactions. (ch. 6)

**Pack:** The pack() method in Tkinter arranges widgets in blocks before placing them in the parent widget. It can arrange widgets horizontally or vertically. (ch. 7)

**Package:** A collection of related modules. (ch. 4)

**Pandas:** A powerful library for data manipulation and analysis, providing data structures like DataFrames to work with structured data easily and efficiently. (ch. 8)

**Parent Class:** See Superclass (ch. 6)

**Place:** The place() method in Tkinter allows for precise control of widget positioning using x and y coordinates. (ch. 7)

**Polymorphism:** The ability of different classes to respond to the same method call in different, but related ways. It allows objects of different classes to be treated as objects of a common superclass. (ch. 6)

**Print Function:** A built-in Python function that outputs text or other data to the console. Example: print("Hello, World!") (ch. 1)

**pyalgotrade:** A Python library for backtesting trading strategies. (ch. 8)

**Pygame:** A set of Python modules designed for writing video games, including computer graphics and sound libraries. (ch. 8)

**PyQt:** A set of Python bindings for Qt libraries used to create cross-platform applications with a native look and feel. (ch. 8)

**Python:** A high-level, interpreted programming language known for its readability and versatility. Python supports multiple programming paradigms, including procedural, object-oriented, and functional programming. (ch. 1)

**Python Script:** A file containing a series of Python commands that can be executed as a program. (ch. 1)

**PyTorch:** An open-source machine learning library based on the Torch library, providing a flexible and dynamic interface for building neural networks. (ch. 8)

**QuantLib:** A library for quantitative finance that provides tools for pricing derivatives, managing portfolios, and more. (ch. 8)

**Scikit-learn:** A library for machine learning that provides simple and efficient tools for data mining and data analysis, built on NumPy, SciPy, and Matplotlib. (ch. 8)

**SciPy:** A Python library used for scientific and technical computing, building on NumPy and providing many functions that operate on NumPy arrays. (ch. 8)

**Scope:** The region of a program where a variable is defined and accessible. (ch. 4)

**Script:** A file containing a series of commands that can be executed as a program. See Python Script (ch. 1)

**Selenium:** A tool for automating web browsers, useful for automated testing of web applications or scraping data from websites. (ch. 8)

**Set:** An unordered collection of unique items. (ch. 3)

**Shell:** See Command Prompt (ch. 1)

**Socket:** A low-level networking interface in Python that provides access to the BSD socket interface, allowing the creation of network connections and data transfer between servers and clients. (ch. 8)

**sorted Function:** Returns a new sorted list from the elements of any iterable. (ch. 4)

**SQL:** Structured Query Language. A standard programming language specifically designed for managing and manipulating relational databases. SQL is used to query, insert, update, and delete data, as well as to create and modify the structure of database systems. (ch. 7)

**String:** A sequence of characters used to represent text in a program. Strings are enclosed in either single or double quotes. Example: "Hello, World!" (ch. 1)

**Subclass:** A class that inherits attributes and methods from another class (superclass or parent class). (ch. 6)

**super() function:** A function used in a subclass to call a method from its superclass. It is often used to extend or modify the behavior of inherited methods. (ch. 6)

**Superclass:** A class whose attributes and methods are inherited by other classes (subclasses or child classes). (ch. 6)

**Syntax:** The set of rules that defines the combinations of symbols that are considered to be a correctly structured program in a programming language. (ch. 1)

**TensorFlow:** An end-to-end open-source platform for machine learning offering a comprehensive ecosystem of tools, libraries, and community resources. (ch. 8)

**Terminal:** See Command Prompt (ch. 1)

**Ternary Conditional Expression:** A shorthand for an if-else statement that returns a value based on a condition. (ch. 2)

**Text:** A Text widget in Tkinter allows for multiline text input. It is versatile for user input and is ideal for applications requiring extensive data entry. (ch. 7)

**Text File:** A file that contains plain text and can be opened and edited with text editors. (ch. 5)

**Tkinter:** Tkinter is Python's standard GUI (Graphical User Interface) toolkit. It allows Python developers to create windows, buttons, text fields, and other widgets to create interactive applications. (ch. 7)

**try/except/finally:** A construct in Python used for handling exceptions and ensuring that cleanup code runs regardless of whether an exception occurred. (ch. 5)

**Tuple:** An immutable ordered collection of items. (ch. 3)

**Type Conversion:** The process of converting one data type to another, such as converting a string to an integer (ch. 2)

**Variable:** A named location in memory used to store data that can be modified during program execution. Example: x = 10 (ch. 1, 2)

**Web Development:** The process of creating websites or web applications. Python is often used on the server-side to handle backend logic, database interactions, and server configuration. Popular frameworks include Django and Flask. (ch. 8)

**While Loop:** Repeats as long as a condition is true. (ch. 3)

**Widget:** A widget is an element of a graphical user interface, such as a button, label, text field, or slider, that users can interact with. (ch. 7)

**with Statement:** A control flow structure in Python that ensures proper acquisition and release of resources, such as file handles. (ch. 5)

**XML File:** eXtensible Markup Language. A markup language that defines a set of rules for encoding documents in a format that is both human-readable and machine-readable. (ch. 5)

**YAML File:** YAML Ain't Markup Language. A human-readable data serialization standard, ideal for configuration files and data processing, known for its readability and support for complex data structures. (ch. 5)

# MORE FROM WIZARDRY PRESS

*Unlocking Artificial Intelligence for Entrepreneur Success!*

Discover how AI can revolutionize your business with this hands-on guide tailored for small businesses and entrepreneurs. Packed with practical playbooks, exercises, and real-world examples, this book demystifies AI and empowers you to harness tools like ChatGPT to save time, spark creativity, and drive growth. Whether you're automating customer service, refining marketing strategies, or exploring innovative ideas, this book offers actionable steps to integrate AI into your workflow. Accessible and engaging, it's the ultimate toolkit for transforming your business with the power of AI.

*Absolute Beginner's Guide to Python Programming*

Dive into the world of programming with this comprehensive and engaging guide to Python, designed for readers with no prior coding experience. From setting up your first Python environment to tackling real-world projects like building games, managing data, and creating graphical user interfaces, this book makes learning Python approachable and fun. Featuring clear explanations, hands-on exercises, and practical projects, you'll develop foundational programming skills and best practices that set you up for success. Whether you're exploring programming as a hobby or looking to kickstart your career, this guide provides the perfect roadmap to mastering Python. Available in both English and Hindi.

*Complete Career Guide for Entry-Level Software Engineers*

Navigate the challenging yet rewarding path of a software engineering career with this all-in-one guide designed for entry-level professionals. From mastering programming fundamentals and understanding industry trends to building soft skills, acing interviews, and thriving in your first job, this book equips you with the tools for success. With practical exercises, expert insights, and actionable advice, you'll learn how to build a strong foundation, craft standout applications, and achieve long-term growth in the tech world. Whether you're just starting or looking to refine your career strategy, this guide is your ultimate roadmap.

# MORE FROM WIZARDRY PRESS

*Absolute Beginner's Guide to SQL Databases*

Master the fundamentals of SQL and unlock the power of relational databases with this hands-on guide tailored for complete beginners. Whether you're an aspiring data analyst, IT professional, or a curious learner, this book takes you step-by-step through setting up databases, writing efficient queries, and avoiding common pitfalls. Learn how to create tables, manage data relationships, and harness SQL's advanced features like joins, CTEs, and query optimization. Packed with real-world examples, practical exercises, and insights into best practices, this guide empowers you to confidently manage data and apply SQL to solve everyday challenges. This guide is perfect for anyone eager to build a strong foundation in database management.

**Please eMail** info@wizardrypress.com **for more information.**

# INDEX

Abstract Base Class, 118, 187
Abstract Class, 118, 122, 187
Abstract Method, 187
API, 119, 144, 159, 187
Arithmetic Operators, 34, 187
BASH, 187
BeautifulSoup, 160, 187
Boolean, 167, 187
break Statement, 187
Button, 127, 128, 129, 134, 135, 137, 138, 142, 143, 144, 148, 149, 153, 155, 177, 178, 187, 188
Callback Function, 135, 138, 140, 141, 187
Child Class, 187
Class, 109, 110, 111, 118, 121, 122, 123, 174, 187, 190
Command Prompt, 187, 191
Comparison Operators, 36, 187
Compiler, 6, 187
Composition, 110, 121, 174, 187
Concatenation, 187
continue Statement, 187
CRUD, 145, 188
CSV File, 188
Data Science, 2, 158, 188
Data Type, 19, 61, 170, 188
Default Button, 188
Dictionary, 60, 63, 64, 65, 169, 188
Django, 1, 2, 7, 158, 188, 192
Duck Typing, 188
Dynamic Typing, 188
Encapsulation, 107, 112, 120, 188
Entry, 104, 135, 136, 137, 138, 145, 148, 149, 177, 178, 188
Environment Variable, 188
Event Loop, 127, 129, 140, 148, 149, 188
except Statement, 188
File Handling, 188
filter Function, 188
finally Statement, 188

Flask, 158, 188, 192
Float, 167, 188
For Loop, 56, 61, 170, 188
format() Method, 24, 25, 188
Frame, 137, 138, 178, 189
Function, 15, 74, 78, 84, 105, 114, 122, 124, 135, 138, 140, 141, 170, 181, 187, 188, 189, 190, 191
Global Variable, 189
Grid, 131, 152, 153, 189
GUI, 80, 116, 117, 125, 127, 128, 133, 137, 141, 143, 144, 148, 149, 150, 151, 152, 153, 154, 156, 161, 188, 189, 191
IDE (Integrated Development Environment), 189
Immutability, 27, 189
Indentation, 30, 189
Inheritance, 113, 114, 115, 120, 121, 175, 189
INI File, 189
Input Function, 189
Integer, 167, 189
Interpreter, 6, 12, 30, 189
JSON, 89, 95, 96, 97, 98, 101, 102, 103, 104, 105, 122, 123, 144, 172, 173, 189
Label, 127, 128, 129, 130, 131, 132, 133, 134, 135, 136, 137, 143, 144, 153, 155, 189
Lambda Function, 75, 76, 77, 79, 142, 172, 189
Layout Manager, 129, 133, 189
List, 60, 63, 64, 65, 149, 168, 177, 189
Local Variable, 189
Logical Operators, 37, 41, 168, 190
Loop, 58, 61, 62, 84, 127, 129, 140, 148, 149, 153, 170, 188, 190, 192
map Function, 190
Message Box, 138, 139, 140, 190
Method Overloading, 115, 190

INDEX

Object-Oriented Programming (OOP), 107, 110, 117, 120, 122
Pack, 130, 190
Polymorphism, 115, 116, 117, 120, 122, 175, 190
Print, 49, 61, 63, 65, 97, 102, 103, 169, 170, 190
Python Standard Library, 93
Scope, 69, 78, 170, 181, 191
Self, 181, 182
Set, 12, 53, 60, 63, 64, 65, 148, 149, 150, 154, 169, 191
String, 21, 24, 41, 167, 189, 191
Subclass, 121, 187, 191
Superclass, 190, 191
Syntax, 30, 31, 113, 191
Tkinter, 80, 125, 126, 127, 128, 129, 130, 131, 132, 133, 138, 140, 141, 142, 143, 144, 145, 146, 147, 148, 149, 150, 151, 152, 153, 154, 156, 161, 187, 188, 189, 190, 191
try/except/finally, 92, 188, 192
Tuple, 63, 64, 65, 192
Type Conversion, 20, 40, 167, 192
Variable, 38, 40, 43, 167, 181, 188, 189, 192
Web Development, 2, 158, 192
While Loop, 58, 61, 170, 192
Widget, 134, 135, 136, 137, 143, 144, 192
with Statement, 90, 192
XML File, 192
YAML File, 192

Made in United States
Cleveland, OH
15 June 2025